Leisure and Lifestyle Retailing

 International Council of Shopping Centers

About the International Council of Shopping Centers

Retailer and shopping center profiles were compiled from myriad sources, including but not limited to information supplied by the retailers or centers themselves, Website data, promotional and press materials and published research findings. The sampling is by no means a complete list of retailers or shopping centers, but instead reflects a representative sampling of excellence in specialty retailing as determined by the editors of this publication. To further convey the retailers' images, photos of stores and merchandise, in addition to samples of advertising and logos, are featured in the retailer profiles. All materials were carefully compiled and edited for consistency in an effort to maintain accurate representation. The editors welcome the readers' input and invite you to send in your comments to:

Publications
International Council of Shopping Centers
1221 Avenue of the Americas
New York, NY 10020-1099

ACKNOWLEDGMENTS
The International Council of Shopping Centers would like to congratulate all of the retailers and shopping centers featured in this book for being selected by our editors for their specialty retail excellence.

We thank all retailers and shopping centers that contributed material, time and expertise in the preparation of this book. We also thank Alberta Davidson, SCMD, and Maria A. Murray for their effort in researching and writing text for the retailer profiles. We also acknowledge ICSC Research Director Michael Baker for writing the shopping center segment and contributing research data to help us better understand this consumer phenomenon.

The International Council of Shopping Centers (ICSC) is the trade association of the shopping center industry. Serving the shopping center industry since 1957, ICSC is a not-for-profit organization with over 43,000 members in 77 countries worldwide.

ICSC members include shopping center

- owners
- developers
- managers
- marketing specialists
- leasing agents
- retailers
- researchers
- attorneys
- architects
- contractors
- consultants
- investors
- lenders and brokers
- academics
- public officials

ICSC holds approximately 200 meetings a year throughout the world and provides a wide array of services and products for shopping center professionals, including publications and research data.

For more information about ICSC, contact:
International Council of Shopping Centers
1221 Avenue of the Americas, 41st Floor
New York, NY 10020-1099
http://www.icsc.org

Published by
INTERNATIONAL COUNCIL OF SHOPPING CENTERS
Publications Department
1221 Avenue of the Americas
New York, NY 10020-1099

Book Design: Harish Patel Design, New York, NY
Cover Design: DK&G Creative Services, New York, NY

ICSC Catalog Number: 223

International Standard Book Number: 1-58268-027-2

Contents

Introduction

Introduction

What's in the Name?

Phrases like "lifestyle retailing" and "leisure retailing" are now firmly entrenched in the retail and shopping center lexicon, but if one takes a step back and thinks about how they got there and what they mean, the answer isn't so obvious. In place of a clearly defined concept of what they represent there are only the names of retailers— Williams-Sonoma, Eddie Bauer, Barnes & Noble, for example—and perhaps a number of familiar mental associations—store-window mannequins dressed in khakis, depicting an air of studied relaxation and self-confidence or artistically crafted appliances and utensils that would look as much at home in an art museum as in a kitchen.

In essence, lifestyle retailers are many of the upscale specialty retailers that operate in malls, lifestyle centers and, in some cases, power centers. Thus, in this book, the terms "lifestyle retailer" and "upscale specialty retailer" will be used interchangeably. These retailers cater to the lifestyles and aspirations of millions of American households with sophisticated tastes for clothing, home furnishings and décor, electronic gadgetry and food, among other things.

Importantly, these households also usually enjoy above-average incomes because the lifestyle retailer competes less on price and more on innovation, both in the merchandise mix and in the shopping experience. This entails greater risk and higher cost, but enables the successful retailer to offer:

- Merchandise that transcends pure functionality to cater to the self-image, aspirations and individuality of a discerning customer.
- An exciting shopping experience that incorporates the best in store design, merchandise layout, lighting, music, video and other in-store entertainment features.

Section IV of this book profiles a number of lifestyle retailers. However, no lifestyle retailer is an island; the shopping center environment in which retailers operate is often as important to the success of the retailers as the stores themselves. Except in rare instances, lifestyle retail stores thrive on their combined drawing power for the discerning shopper interested in creating an outfit, a wardrobe, a kitchen or a child's bedroom.

Although there were approximately 75 true lifestyle centers in the country as of the end of 2002, they are immensely varied.

Take size, for example, which varies from the tiny One Pacific Place in Omaha, Nebraska (90,000 sf) to the 760,000 sf Summit Shopping Center in Birmingham, Alabama. In some, the role of sit-down dining is minimal (The Grove at Shrewsbury in Shrewsbury, New Jersey, has just one table-service restaurant), while in others, such as Reston Town Center in Reston, Virginia, with 15 restaurants, it is paramount. About half of the centers have cinemas, half don't. Most rely heavily on national chain specialty retailers, but some don't. For example,

Mizner Park in Boca Raton, Florida, has a Chico's and a Banana Republic, but, beyond those it is dependent mostly on local tenants. Some are pure retail projects, while others, such as Redmond Town Center in Redmond, Washington, are mixed-use centers, with office, residential, hotel and other uses.

Lifestyle centers often border on entertainment centers, theme/festival centers, open-air regional malls and other shopping center types.

The bottom line is that these centers do not adhere to a cookie-cutter approach and some border on entertainment centers, theme/festival centers, open-air regional malls and other shopping center types. Each center is fairly unique, and in this uniqueness lies some of the appeal. However, at the heart of each center is the important commonality of the upscale specialty, or "lifestyle," retailer.

This book is organized as follows: Section I provides an overview of the history and development of the lifestyle center. Section II provides case studies of five lifestyle centers. Section III provides a consumer viewpoint on lifestyle centers. Section IV provides profiles of lifestyle retailers.

Section I

A Brief History of the Lifestyle Center

A Brief History of the Lifestyle Center

The Struggle for Acceptance

The term "lifestyle center" was first coined about 15 years ago by Poag & McEwen Lifestyle Centers Inc., whose first center of that genre—The Shops of Saddle Creek, in Germantown, Tennessee—opened in 1987. Although Poag & McEwen pioneered both the name and the genre, there are centers pre-dating Saddle Creek that also qualify for the moniker of "lifestyle center." These include Lincoln Square Shopping Center (opened in 1983) in Arlington, Texas and two centers that opened in 1985: Arboretum at Great Hills in Austin, Texas, and Old Hyde Park Village in downtown Tampa, Florida. The following year, University Park Village in Fort Worth, Texas, and Preston Park Village in Plano, Texas, both opened. (It should be noted, however, that University Park Village probably qualified as a true lifestyle center when it changed ownership and was revitalized in 1994. It reopened in its current 172,000 sf format in 1995.)

Financing has traditionally been a huge hurdle in the development of the concept, particularly in the early days of the mid-1980's when anchorless centers were more of an unknown entity. On account of their heavy landscaping and architectural features, lifestyle centers' development costs are typically more akin to those of a mall than a conventional strip center. Lenders were skeptical about the economics of an unanchored center that cost $200 per sf to build, and today generally put up no more than two-thirds of the funding, even with higher interest rates.

To overcome financing problems and spread risk, some developers have teamed up with partners. For example, Poag & McEwen joined forces with a large shopping center real estate investment trust, Developers Diversified Realty, to finance and develop Deer Park Town Center in Chicago, which opened in 2000.

One of the problems with many of the early failed lifestyle center development attempts was that they retained the mall configuration of stores facing inward away from the street. They were, in essence, roofless and anchorless malls, thus foregoing both the potential traffic generated by an anchor *and* the greater convenience of street parking immediately in front of store entrances.

There were other problems as well, including poor location and too much emphasis on local tenants who were not sufficiently resilient over the long haul. The reliance on local tenants was, in turn, due largely to the reluctance of the national chains to venture out from the shadows of the department stores in their familiar regional mall locations.

Community opposition has also been a hurdle in some instances, particularly where the viability of the proposed center depended upon infrastructure enhancements, such as widening an existing road or building a new one. More often than not, such opposition has been quieted when skeptics saw the unique qualities and economic benefits of the completed center.

Some of the doubts about the economic viability of lifestyle centers have been gradually overcome as the key determinants to the success or failure of a lifestyle center have become clearer and as many of the key players have demonstrated a successful track record. The basis for the success of the centers has been shopper acceptance. Shopper attitudes are discussed in detail in Section III of this book, beginning on page 47.

Pioneer Lifestyle Centers: 1983–1992

Although momentum in construction of new lifestyle centers has only really picked up in the past five or six years, the genre began to put down fairly solid roots in the 1980's, beginning with the aforementioned openings of Lincoln Square, Arboretum at Great Hills and Old Hyde Park Village.

Lincoln Square is one of the centers featured in Section II. Arboretum, a 193,000 sf center with about 40 stores, three restaurants and a seven-screen cinema, opened in Austin, Texas, within four miles of the area's dominant upscale mall—Highland Mall—and six miles from the more "moderate" Barton Creek Mall. The origi-

Deer Park Town Center is the result of a partnership between Poag & McEwen and REIT Developers Diversified Realty.

nal tenants at Arboretum were more local and independent, largely pulled from Austin's deteriorated downtown business district. (Austin was in the throes of serious economic difficulties because of the savings and loan debacle.)

One of the founding tenants of Arboretum was the Scarborough department store, which went out of business in 1988. This was a seminal point for the center, whose owners subdivided the vacant department store space to make room for the upscale national chains that wanted to move into the center.

By the mid-1990's, nationals such as Limited Brand's Express, Victoria's Secret and Bath & Body Works, Williams-Sonoma's Pottery Barn and Gap Inc.'s Banana Republic and Gap were established in the center.

Meanwhile, Old Hyde Park Village opened south of downtown Tampa, Florida, in the historic Hyde Park district. Spanning about a half-dozen blocks of tree-lined streets, the center now boasts about 60 retail stores, five restaurants and, like Arboretum, a cinema.

Two more lifestyle center openings, including Shops of Saddle Creek, in Germantown, Tennessee, took place in each of the following two years. Saddle Creek, which commenced operating 100%-leased in April 1987, initially consisted of 84,000 sf of gross leasable area (GLA). A 38,000 sf extension— Saddle Creek South—began operation with the opening of a Talbots store in May 1989.

There was a lull in new openings in 1988, and then two more openings—One Pacific Place, Omaha, Nebraska and The Grove at Shrewsbury, Shrewsbury, New Jersey—in 1989. Both of these cen-

Arboretum made room for upscale national tenants, when Scarborough department store went out of business.

A flurry of lifestyle center openings occurred in the early 1990's.

ters are interesting in their own way. One Pacific Place, with 90,000 sf of retail GLA and about 25 stores, is probably the smallest lifestyle center in existence. The Grove at Shrewsbury, as noted earlier, is distinctive for its minimal reliance on food service as a customer draw, with only one table-service restaurant.

There were a flurry of lifestyle center openings in the early 1990's. Reston Town Center, Bradley Fair, CocoWalk, Mizner Park and Town Square Center all debuted during the recessionary period of 1990–92.

Three of the centers—CocoWalk, Mizner Park and Reston Town Center—are particularly notable for their entertainment offerings. CocoWalk, located in downtown Coconut Grove, Florida, has a

16-screen cinema, restaurants and bars that keep the center open until 10 p.m. on weeknights and midnight on the weekends. (The restaurants and bars stay open until 2 a.m.)

Mizner Park, in Boca Raton, Florida, houses the Boca Raton Museum of Art, an 1,800-seat concert hall and an amphitheater. It also has an eight-screen movie theater.

Meanwhile, Reston Town Center, in Reston, Virginia, boasts an ice-skating pavilion with a glass roof that doubles as an outdoor entertainment venue in the warm seasons. Events hosted include a summer concert series and Northern Virginia Fine Arts Festival. To round off the entertainment offering, Reston Town Center also has a 13-screen cinema.

The Concept Multiplies

From 1993 through 1995, there were no new lifestyle center openings. However, beginning in 1996, the concept took off with two more openings, including the largest lifestyle center to that point and still among the largest to this day—Town Center Plaza in Leawood, Kansas.

Five more openings occurred in 1997 alone and 29 in the five years from 1997 to 2002.

About 25 more are on the drawing board for opening in the 2003–2004 time frame. The rapid expansion of the concept during the past five years is partly due to consumer acceptance (Section III of this book examines this in detail) and also greater acceptance by the specialty retail chains.

Some leisure centers rely on national chain specialty retailers, while others have a mix of national and local tenants.

Retailers may be drawn to lifestyle centers due to lower occupancy costs resulting from lower common area maintenance (CAM) and utility costs.

Retailers are warming to these centers for a number of reasons:

- First, the upscale nature of the trade areas makes them attractive locations with or without an anchor, provided that there is a critical mass of other specialty retailers.

- Second, as noted earlier, regional mall openings have almost ground to a complete halt, leaving growth-minded retailers with a limited number of options for expanding their store bases.

- Third, occupancy costs may often be lower in a lifestyle center than in an upscale mall, partly because of lower common area maintenance (CAM) and utility costs.

- Fourth, lifestyle retailers have become more proficient at making themselves destinations. This is partly a function of the "clustering" of the retailers themselves, but it is increasingly due to each retailer's own traffic-driving initiatives. This is worth pausing to examine in more detail because it provides part of the basis for challenging the traditional assumption that a shopping center without anchors, or with weak anchors, will not work.

Managing Without an Anchor— Customer Relationship Management (CRM)

Specialty retailers are increasing their investments in marketing and Customer Relationship Management (CRM) initiatives to drive traffic. Initiatives can take several different forms, such as the following:

- *Loyalty programs.* These programs provide incentives for good customers to visit the store more often. They often involve proprietary credit cards and selective targeting of customers for promotions via catalogs, magalogs and other mailings. A good example of a loyalty program is Chico's Passport Club. Membership is conferred on shoppers who sign up and then spend $500 at the store. Member benefits include a 5% discount on purchases, birthday bonuses and invitations to special events (such as private parties and unique shopping opportunities), which themselves serve to enhance customer loyalty.

Another example of a loyalty program is Talbots' Classic Awards, in which shoppers receive a $25 "dividend" (credit towards another purchase) for every $500 of purchases made on the Talbots' charge card, birthday bonuses and other special offers.

- *Catalogs.* Apart from their function as an independent revenue generator and as a testing ground for new products prior to full store rollout, catalog mailings are a tried and tested way of driving traffic to stores. One lifestyle retailer, Restoration Hardware, now mails its catalogs exclusively in markets where it has stores.

- *Direct Mail (including e-mail).* Direct mail and e-mail programs allow the same kind of customer targeting but at significantly less cost than catalogs. A large number of specialty retailers now regularly use e-mail to keep customer attention on the brand and drive traffic to stores. For example, Limited Brands' Bath & Body Works mailed an invitation to customers to visit a Bath & Body Works store and pick up a free sample of the True Blue Spa line.

Regular mailings are generally more expensive than e-mail but offer additional versatility. For instance, another Limited Brands concept, Victoria's Secret, recently mailed select customers a free Body by Victoria panty.

As lifestyle retailers continue to refine these marketing techniques, they should become increasingly independent of the need to ply their trade in the shadows of one or more large anchor stores. It should be emphasized, however, that marketing and brand enhancement by themselves will not do the trick entirely—clustering together in a shopping center, whether it be a mall or lifestyle center, is generally critical to making lifestyle retailers an independent destination for shoppers.

The Lifestyle Center Openings Timeline

1983	Lincoln Square Shopping Center	Arlington, TX	450,000 sf
1984–1985	Arboretum at Great Hills	Austin, TX	193,000 sf
	Old Hyde Park Village	Tampa, FL	248,000 sf
1986	Preston Park Village	Plano, TX	269,000 sf
	University Park Village	Fort Worth, TX	172,000 sf
1987	Bayside Marketplace	Miami, FL	227,000 sf
	The Shops of Saddle Creek	Germantown, TN	143,000 sf
1988–1989	One Pacific Place	Omaha, NE	90,000 sf
	The Grove at Shrewsbury	Shrewsbury, NJ	145,000 sf
1990	Reston Town Center	Reston, VA	250,000 sf
	Bradley Fair Shopping Center	Wichita, KS	220,000 sf
	CocoWalk	Coconut Grove, FL	163,000 sf
1991	Mizner Park	Boca Raton, FL	236,000 sf
1992	Town Square Center	Wheaton, IL	179,000 sf
1996	The Promenade at Westlake	Thousand Oaks, CA	202,000 sf
	Town Center Plaza	Leawood, KS	700,000 sf
1997	University Village	Seattle, WA	400,000 sf
	Redmond Town Center	Redmond, WA	569,000 sf
	The Summit Shopping Center	Birmingham, AL	760,000 sf
	Huebner Oaks	San Antonio, TX	380,000 sf
	Alamo Quarry Marketplace	San Antonio, TX	585,000 sf

1998	The Commons at Calabasas	Calabasas, CA	198,000 sf
	The Shops at Riverwoods	Provo, UT	193,000 sf
	Gardens on El Paseo	Palm Desert, CA	200,000 sf
	Denver Pavilions	Denver, CO	350,000 sf
1999	The Avenue of the Peninsula	Rolling Hills Estates, CA	374,000 sf
	The Shops at Sunset Place	South Miami, FL	506,000 sf
	The Avenue® East Cobb	Marietta, GA	225,000 sf
	Southlake Town Square	Southlake, TX	201,000 sf
	Mt. Pleasant Towne Center	Mt. Pleasant, SC	427,000 sf
	SouthPointe Pavilions	Lincoln, NE	500,000 sf
2000	Centro Ybor	Tampa, FL	214,000 sf
	Palladium at City Place	West Palm Beach, FL	600,000 sf
	Rookwood Commons	Norwood, OH	326,000 sf
	Deer Park Town Center	Deer Park, IL	506,000 sf
2001	Jefferson Pointe	Ft. Wayne, NJ	562,000 sf
	Old Mill District at River Bend	Bend, OR	150,000 sf
	The Shoppes at Brinton Lakes	Glen Mills, PA	153,000 sf
	The Summit Louisville	Louisville, KY	368,000 sf
	Aspen Grove	Littleton, CO	244,000 sf
2002	Geneva Commons	Geneva, IL	419,000 sf
	Fountain Walk	Novi, MI	737,000 sf
	The Grove at Farmers Market	Los Angeles, CA	575,000 sf
	Village of Rochester Hills	Rochester Hills, MI	375,000 sf
	Eastwood Town Center	Lansing, MI	393,000 sf

Section II

Case Studies

Aspen Grove

Aspen Grove, developed by Poag & McEwen in partnership with Developers Diversified Realty, is one of the more recent additions to the ranks of lifestyle centers and yet is the first one in the state of Colorado. Opened in November 2001 at the foot of the Rocky Mountains in Littleton, Aspen Grove is adjacent to The Polo Reserve (a high-end residential development), Platte River Park and a new rapid-transit system connecting the area with downtown Denver.

The center, which has about 244,000 sf of GLA, is rich in the architectural and landscaping features that are typical of lifestyle centers, including fountains, benches and trees. The buildings themselves are of a bucolic stone and wood in deference to Colorado's architectural heritage. Other commercial developments, including offices and hotels, add to the strong local demographics to provide an extensive and affluent customer base.

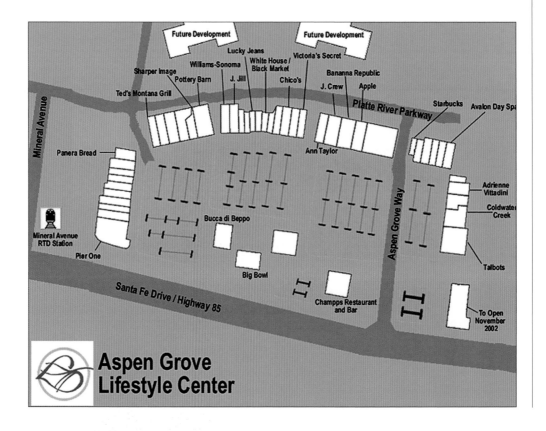

Aspen Grove, at the foot of Colorado's Rocky Mountains, has about 244,000 sf of GLA.

The center is rich in architectural and landscaping features, which are typical of lifestyle centers.

Aspen Grove's tenant mix doesn't include any department store anchors or bookstores, but it features a number of retailers' first stores in Colorado, including Adrienne Vittadini, Apple Computer, Aeropostale and Coconuts. These join an impressive lineup of upscale specialty retailers such as Ann Taylor, Banana Republic, Chico's, Talbots, Pottery Barn and J. Crew. In all, there are over 50 stores and restaurants. Restaurants are both full-service and quick-service, indoor and outdoor.

The tenant mix does not include any department store anchors or bookstores, but it features a number of retailers' first stores in Colorado, including Adrienne Vittadini and Apple Computer, among others.

The nearest upscale mall, Park Meadows, is about eight miles away and many of the tenants there also have stores at Aspen Grove. Only a handful of tenants at Park Meadows declined to come to Aspen Grove because of sales transfer concerns—most thought they needed to be in both centers.

Although Aspen Grove is intended to be a pleasant place to while away some time, the U-shaped layout with ample parking immediately in front of stores enhances the convenience and efficiency of a shopping trip. Shoppers can park close to their desired retailers and complete the trip relatively quickly if they so choose.

There are over 50 stores and restaurants in the center.

The Avenue® East Cobb

The Avenue® East Cobb, which opened in August 1999, is a 225,000 sf lifestyle center located near the intersection of State Highway 120 and Johnson Ferry Road in metropolitan Atlanta's fast-growing Cobb County.

Although the center strives primarily for pedestrian-friendly comfort and convenience, there is a suggestion of lavishness and even opulence in the elaborate landscaping and architectural features, which include brick pedestrian walkways, bronze statues, an outdoor amphitheater, ornamental lamps,

*The Avenue®
East Cobb is a
225,000 sf center
in metropolitan
Atlanta's fast-
growing Cobb
County.*

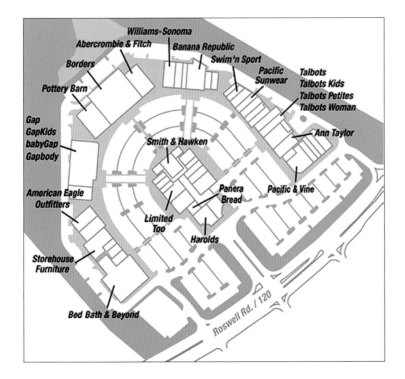

The center strives for pedestrian-friendly comfort and convenience by using brick walkways and ornamental lamps.

stamped stone passages and unique and varying storefront designs.

The center sits on a 30-acre site and cost approximately $43 million to develop. It was a significant challenge for the developer, Cousins Properties Inc. of Atlanta, Georgia, to assemble the whole 30-acre parcel, as it involved acquisition of 14 separately owned residences and a 16-acre driving range. Also, the whole site needed to be rezoned. Since it affected individuals' residences, emotions were high, yet the issues were resolved satisfactorily to all concerned in the space of 14 months.

All told, the center has about 50 retail stores arranged on both sides of a U-shaped driveway. The demographics of East Cobb and the surrounding areas are extremely appealing—there are about 69,000 households in the five-mile ring with an average income of $126,000. This has enabled Cousins to overcome initial retailer skepticism about their prospects in a nonanchored open-air center

Williams-Sonoma, Gap and Banana Republic are among the 50 retailers in the center.

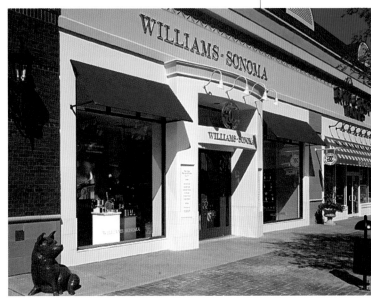

and attract a strong roster of national merchants. (When the center opened for business it had 20 tenants, but the roster quickly expanded to its current size as retailers sitting on the fence decided they couldn't afford to be left out.) Thus, among the center's retail attractions are Abercrombie & Fitch, Banana Republic, Bed Bath & Beyond, Talbots and Victoria's Secret. There are three table-service restaurants and no fast food.

Residents of Cobb County have historically lacked the close availability of quality retailers in an upscale environment. With the development of The Avenue® East Cobb, they have access to outdoor and fine dining, national and local retailers and a community "town center." The Avenue has become a community gathering place, where patrons watch performances and listen to book readings in the amphitheater, attend cooking demonstrations or meet with friends and family to shop and dine.

This nonanchored open-air center includes the Ann Taylor store in its retail attractions.

The Gardens on El Paseo

The Gardens on El Paseo, developed by Madison Marquette, is an oasis in the form of a $60 million lifestyle center in Southern California's scorching Coachella Valley, where temperatures routinely reach 100-plus degrees in summer. The center's two-story buildings are arranged around an outdoor plaza, and its design elements, which include high walls, trellises, plentiful indigenous plants and water features, are cool to the eye and in harmony with the desert environment.

The Gardens on El Paseo is a $60 million lifestyle center located in Southern California.

The center opened in November 1998 and in the first five years of its existence has solidified its status as a community meeting place for locals and a magnet for tourists. The Gardens includes a blend of national stores such as Ann Taylor, Brooks Brothers, Talbots, Sharper Image and a Saks Fifth Avenue department store, as well as upscale local merchants and restaurants largely unavailable anywhere else within a 60-mile radius.

Apart from being a unique shopping environment, The Gardens is a venue for special events and high-caliber entertainment. For example, it hosts a 12-week concert series benefiting 12 nonprofit organizations, fashion shows and other events throughout the year.

The Gardens includes a blend of national stores, such as Saks Fifth Avenue and Banana Republic, as well as upscale local merchants and restaurants.

The center's two-story buildings are enhanced by design elements that include plentiful indigenous plants and water features.

Similar to most lifestyle centers, The Gardens enjoys a trading area with upscale demographics. The center is most effective in drawing year-round residents aged 35 and older with incomes above $75,000, including a slightly older clientele earning over $100,000.

The center also attracts affluent tourists—the Coachella Valley's location and climate have created a first-class international resort that is easily accessible by freeway, rail or air from anywhere in the United States, Canada or Mexico. The influx of snowbirds and winter visitors is important to center merchants for six months of the year. Visitors to the area also include a younger set who travel from Los Angeles and San Diego for a week or weekend getaway of shopping, nightlife, golf, tennis and hiking.

However, while tourists are important for six months, the year-round residents are most critical in ensuring the success of The Gardens' merchants. The Coachella Valley is a very fast-growing area and continues to attract educated and sophisticated full- and part-time residents from surrounding Southern California regions, which is resulting in a steady decrease in the average age of the resident population. The influx is also driving up the price of real estate, which hit a record high in 2000.

The Gardens doesn't have the Coachella Valley all to itself from a shopping standpoint—the 850,000 sf Westfield Shoppingtown Palm Desert is just five miles away and another upscale open-air center, the 200,000 sf River at Rancho Mirage, is 10 miles away. However, the merchandising and characteristics of each center are sufficiently distinct that the centers are complementary destinations with significant cross-shopping activity.

The merchandising and characteristics of the center make it sufficiently distinct from nearby centers.

Lincoln Square Shopping Center

LINCOLN SQUARE

Lincoln Square Shopping Center is adjacent to I-30 in Arlington, Texas, linked to an "entertainment district" that includes The Ballpark in Arlington (home to the Texas Rangers and Six Flags Over Texas), both within half a mile of the center. The center, which was developed by Lincoln Square Property Company and is co-owned by Transwestern Investment Co. and Dunhill Partners, has 450,000 sf of GLA and sits on a 52-acre site.

The center was developed in two phases, with the first opened for business in 1983 and the second in 1984. There were few problems with respect to site acquisition—it was a greenfield development already zoned for retail use—although a road that divides the first and second phases of the center needed to be extended for Phase II to be viable. Further redevelopment is on the drawing board, involving the closure of a nursery at the far western edge of the center and the introduction of some big-box retailers.

Lincoln Square Shopping Center, in Arlington, Texas, has 450,000 sf of GLA and sits on a 52-acre site.

Landscaping features add an attractive touch.

Lincoln Square's 50-plus stores are an eclectic blend of national chains—including Gap, Chico's, Talbots, Bath & Body Works and Pier 1 Imports—and local independents. The center also offers a wide range of eating options with 14 table-service restaurants and five eateries.

The center exhibits a wide repertoire of architectural and landscaping features, including fountains, sculptures, trees and gaslights. Heavy emphasis was placed on the materials used in construction. The roofs are constructed out of genuine English slate, which interestingly was purchased from the owners of a separate mixed-use project underway in downtown Dallas at the same time as Lincoln Square was being built.

The Lincoln Square area has solid demographics, with an average household income of almost $62,000 and more than 102,000 households in the five-mile ring. It also has limited competition—The Parks at Arlington is the nearest mall and that is more than 10 miles away.

The relatively young median age of the center's clientele—about 30—is partly attributable to heavy patronage from students at the nearby campus of the University of Texas. The center also leverages its proximity to The Ballpark to host customers in need of dining and shopping before and after the game.

The center exhibits a wide range of architectural and décor features.

Lincoln Square is also striving to benefit more from the tourist trade—it is connected directly by trolley bus to The Ballpark, Six Flags and 28 local hotels. As an extra sweetener to the tourists, Lincoln Square offers a coupon book that can be picked up at the front desks of local hotels.

One Pacific Place

One Pacific Place in Omaha, Nebraska, has the distinction of being probably the smallest lifestyle center there is. However, with just 90,366 sf of GLA sitting on a 10.5-acre site, the diminutive center with its contemporary architectural style packs a big punch in terms of its retail draw.

The center opened for business in 1989. However, making the project happen in the first place was not all smooth sailing for the developers, Poag & McEwen. One Pacific Place is built on what was virtually the only remaining farmland in the area and the local community initially had reservations about it. A compromise was struck in which the developers—who had ambitions for a bigger retail development than the one that materialized—agreed to allow the surrounds to remain in government

One Pacific Place in Omaha, Nebraska, has just 90,366 sf of GLA sitting on a 10.5-acre site, making it one of the smallest lifestyle centers.

The center's trading area demographics are well-matched to the center's target customers.

Adjoining office and residential developments form a "node" with the center that has become a model for the area's other developments.

The center is a unique and attractive retail venue for shoppers.

Several restaurants are included in the center's tenant mix.

hands and be maintained as parkland in return for permission to build the center on its current 10-plus-acre site.

At around the same time as the retail center went up, three office buildings rose on adjacent land. A few years later a large residential development also emerged nearby. Both the office workers and the local residents offer significant spending power for the center's retailers. In fact, One Pacific Place and the adjoining office and residential developments form a "node" that became the poster child for Omaha metropolitan planning in the early 1990's. The city planners wanted to create more such nodes in order to stop suburban sprawl and enable people to walk more and drive less to do their jobs, shop and be entertained.

One Pacific Place's tenant roster is quintessentially that of a lifestyle center. Its stores include Abercrombie & Fitch, Ann Taylor, Bath & Body Works, The Bombay Company and a number of other upscale specialty retailers, in addition to several restaurants.

The center's trading area demographics are well-matched to the stores' target customers. There are approximately 108,000 households in the five-mile ring with an average income of $79,383. About 38 percent of the households have incomes over $75,000 and more than 20 percent have incomes above $100,000. Even with these good local demographics, the center's management estimates that almost 10 percent of its business comes from beyond the trading area, indicating an extraordinary regional draw for a center of such modest size.

The tenant roster reflects that of many lifestyle centers, including stores such as Gap.

The center's management estimates that almost 10 percent of its business comes from beyond its trading area.

One Pacific Place is not the only shopping opportunity for area residents—Oak View Mall, a middle-market mall with 865,000 sf of GLA, is about three miles away, and Regency Court, a high-end enclosed specialty center actively bringing in national tenants, is only two miles away. Moreover, another lifestyle center is on the drawing board for a location about five miles from One Pacific Place. Regardless of burgeoning competition, One Pacific Place remains a unique and attractive shopping venue and a great early example of the lifestyle center genre.

Section III

Lifestyle Center Shopper Profile

Lifestyle Center Shopper Profile

ICSC studied the profile of the lifestyle center shopper in detail in a consumer study conducted in 2002. The study was devised to meet the following research objectives:

- Determine lifestyle center trip characteristics, such as trip purpose, duration and frequency, number of stores visited and amount spent on retail items and food and drink.

- Develop a package of shopper demographics, including age, income, presence of children at home, education and gender.

- Determine the specific stores shoppers like most at each center.

- Obtain shoppers' of lifestyle centers vis-à-vis competing regional malls on such factors as convenience, tenant mix, quality levels, merchandise variety, price emphasis, shopping atmosphere, safety and security and parking.

- Determine the characteristics of lifestyle centers' trade areas.

The study consisted of intercept surveys of 1,500 shoppers at five representative lifestyle centers across the country and was conducted by Consumer Research Corporation of Minneapolis, MN. The centers were:

- Arboretum at Great Hills: Austin, TX; 193,000 sf; opened 1985.
- Aspen Grove: Littleton, CO; 243,900 sf; opened 2001.
- The Avenue® East Cobb: Marietta, GA; 225,000 sf; opened 1999.
- Deer Park Town Center: Deer Park, IL; 506,000 sf; opened 2000.
- Huebner Oaks: San Antonio, TX; 380,000 sf; opened 1997.

The average number of sit-down restaurants at the centers was three, two centers had movie theaters nearby and the total number of stores ranged from 43 to 60. Average sales per square foot (psf) for the centers in 2001 (excluding Aspen Grove, which was not open for the full year) were $325 (including anchors), $408 psf (without anchors).

The interviews were conducted with lifestyle center shoppers aged 18 years or older who were not employed at the center and who had completed their shopping visit to the center. A total of 300 interviews were conducted at each of the five centers included in the study.

Shoppers were selected at random, and the interviews were balanced by day of week and time of day to achieve a representative sample of customers. Interviews took place over a seven-day period at each center so that weekday, weeknight and weekend shoppers were represented in the trade area definition and the shopper profiles. The majority of the interviewing took place September 19–29, 2002. (The only exception is that 180 of the 300 interviews conducted at the Aspen Grove center took place June 24–30, 2002.)

Lifestyle Center Shopping Trip Characteristics

The following are basic data from the consumer study on lifestyle center trip frequency, purpose, duration and spending. The lifestyle center data are compared in each case with the ICSC benchmark for regional shopping centers for the years 2000–2001.

PURPOSE AND DURATION OF VISITS TO LIFESTYLE CENTER

Three-fourths (74%) of lifestyle center shoppers came to the center either to visit a specific store or shop for a specific item. A further 30% came to browse and 9% came to eat. (The percentages add to more than 100 because multiple responses were allowed.)

Two of the centers had a relatively high percentage of browsers, while the other three had an overwhelming majority of purpose-driven shoppers. (**See Figure 1.**)

Comparing the lifestyle center data to the ICSC benchmark for regional shopping centers in **Figure 1** suggests that the lifestyle center trip

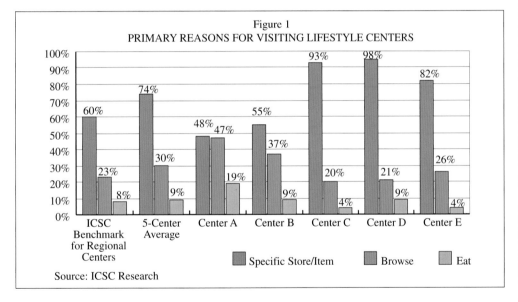

Figure 1
PRIMARY REASONS FOR VISITING LIFESTYLE CENTERS

Source: ICSC Research

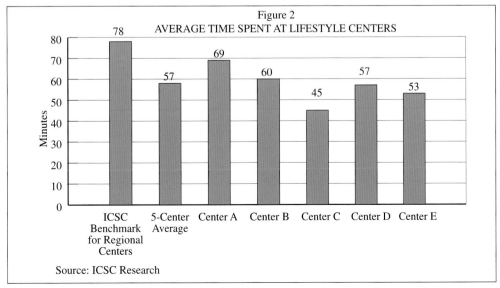

Figure 2
AVERAGE TIME SPENT AT LIFESTYLE CENTERS

Source: ICSC Research

was generally a more purpose-driven one. This was supported by data on trip duration, which showed that the average duration for the lifestyle centers was only 57 minutes, significantly lower than the average mall visit of approximately 78 minutes, or 73 minutes for malls with GLA under 800,000 square feet. **(See Figure 2.)** The average trip duration for lifestyle center shoppers originating in the core trade area was 54 minutes, while those from outside the trade area averaged 62 minutes.

Shoppers at the two centers with the highest proportion of browsers also reported a longer average duration of visit (69 minutes and 60 minutes, respectively).

STORE VISITS AND BUYER CONVERSION RATES

Lifestyle center shoppers visited an average of 2.9 retail stores per trip. **(See Figure 3.)** One center (with 4.3 store visits) skewed the results upward. Excluding this center, the average was 2.6 stores per visit, closer to the regional center benchmark of 2.3.

Purchases across the five centers were made at an average of 1.2 stores, which was the same as for regional malls **(Figure 3)**. However, the average conversion ratio of 0.41 was lower than for malls because the lifestyle center shoppers visited more stores.

The conversion ratio varied across the five centers, ranging from 0.30 to 0.50. The center with the lowest conversation ratio was also the center with the highest proportion of browsers and highest number of per-shopper store visits.

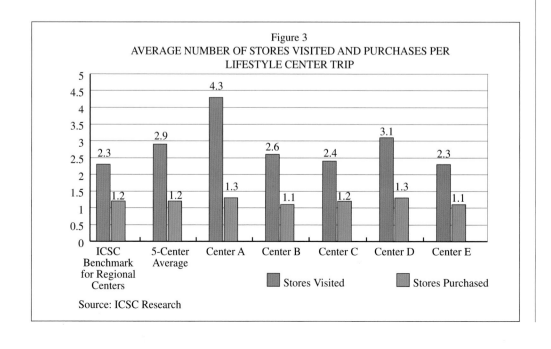

Figure 3
AVERAGE NUMBER OF STORES VISITED AND PURCHASES PER
LIFESTYLE CENTER TRIP

Source: ICSC Research

AVERAGE EXPENDITURES

The average lifestyle center expenditure per trip at retail stores was $75.70, a figure closely in keeping with the ICSC regional mall benchmark. **(See Figure 4.)** The center whose core trade area had the highest average household income and the highest percentage of households with incomes above $75,000 enjoyed the highest retail expenditure per trip of $122.30. Excluding this center, the average retail expenditure per trip was $64.08.

Average expenditure per trip on food and drink at the five lifestyle centers was $4.10, slightly below the ICSC regional mall benchmark of $4.70. The center with the highest percentage of browsers and the longest average trip duration among its clientele enjoyed relatively higher expenditures on food and drink ($7.50 per trip).

Thus, average spending on all items for the lifestyle centers was $79.80. Dividing $79.80 by the average visit duration of 57 minutes yields shopper productivity of $84.00 per hour, which compares favorably with $57.70 per hour for regional centers.

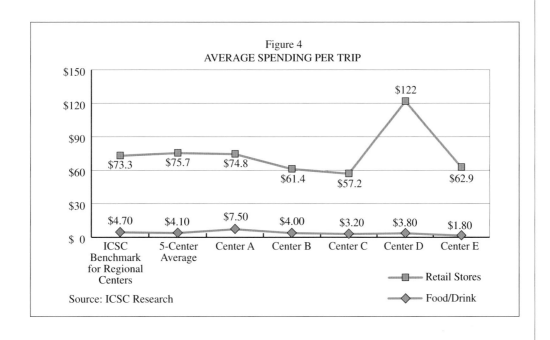

Figure 4
AVERAGE SPENDING PER TRIP

Source: ICSC Research

Figures 5, 6 and 7 break out lifestyle center expenditures by age group, income group and shopper origin, respectively. Average spending per trip increased markedly with income, which, in turn, was associated with the prime earnings years of 35-64. Spending at both the stores and eating establishments was greatest among those originating outside of the trade area. There was little difference in spending between shoppers originating in the core trade area and those originating in the secondary trade area.

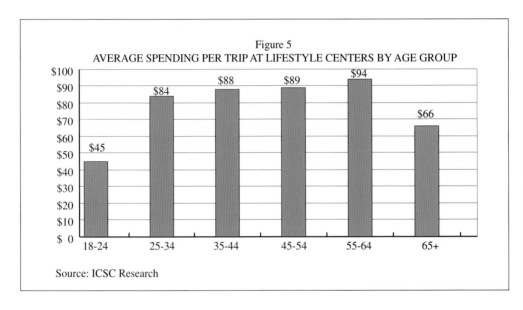

Figure 5
AVERAGE SPENDING PER TRIP AT LIFESTYLE CENTERS BY AGE GROUP

Source: ICSC Research

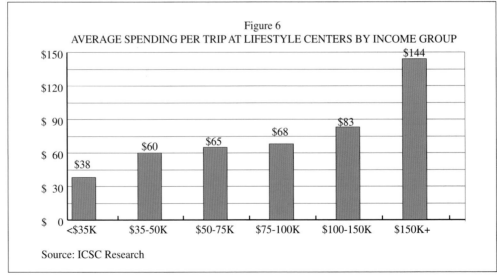

Figure 6
AVERAGE SPENDING PER TRIP AT LIFESTYLE CENTERS BY INCOME GROUP

Source: ICSC Research

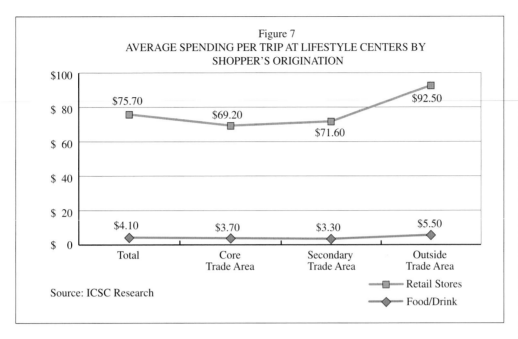

Figure 7
AVERAGE SPENDING PER TRIP AT LIFESTYLE CENTERS BY
SHOPPER'S ORIGINATION

Source: ICSC Research

SHOPPING FREQUENCY

Lifestyle center shoppers visited the center an average of 3.8 times during the last 30 days, or roughly once a week. This compared with 3.4 visits per 30 days for regional centers. Note that there was significant variance across the five lifestyle centers, with a range of 2.8–4.9 trips per 30 days.

The average number of visits declined from 4.6 for shoppers in the core trade area to 2.6 for shoppers outside the trade area. (**See Figure 8.**) This big trip frequency advantage for customers in the core trade area more than compensated for their lower average per-trip expenditures (**Figure 7**) and caused them to spend more over the course of the 30-day period than shoppers outside the trade area.

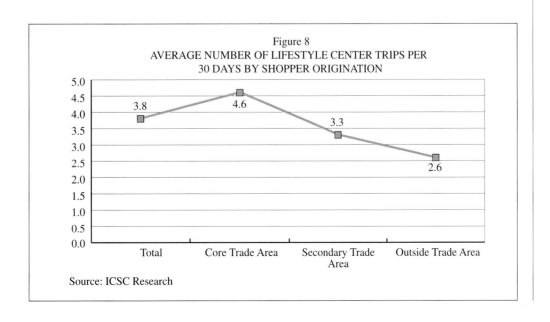

Figure 8
AVERAGE NUMBER OF LIFESTYLE CENTER TRIPS PER
30 DAYS BY SHOPPER ORIGINATION

Source: ICSC Research

Survey respondents at the lifestyle centers were also asked specifically to state how frequently they had visited their favorite regional center in the last 30 days. The average trip frequency was 2.5, with 19% of the shoppers saying they had no favorite regional center or had made no trips to their favorite regional center during the most recent 30 days. **(See Figure 9.)** These data indicated that lifestyle center shoppers had for the most part not forsaken the mall; rather, they were likely to be mall shoppers as well as lifestyle center shoppers.

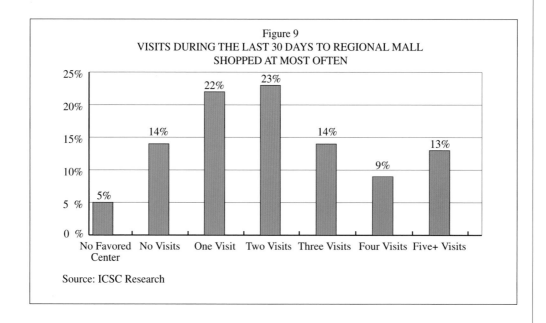

Figure 9
VISITS DURING THE LAST 30 DAYS TO REGIONAL MALL
SHOPPED AT MOST OFTEN

Source: ICSC Research

Shoppers' Perceptions of Lifestyle Centers

Shoppers were asked to rate eight attributes of lifestyle centers, ranging from poor to excellent. The results are presented in **Table 1.**

For each of the eight attributes, shoppers were also asked whether the lifestyle center was better than, the same as or worse than their favorite regional center. The results are presented in **Table 2.**

Overall, the majority of respondents rated three attributes of the lifestyle centers better than their favorite regional mall: overall atmosphere and shopping environment, convenience of parking and convenience of the location in relation to where they lived. However, two-thirds of the respondents said the quality of the merchandise at the lifestyle centers and the prices for the quality offered were the same as their favorite mall.

Table 1. Average Ratings by Shoppers of Lifestyle Center Attributes

	Average Rating (5-Point Scale)
Feelings of safety and security	4.8
Overall atmosphere and shopping environment	4.7
Quality of merchandise	4.7
Convenience of getting from store to store	4.5
Convenience of parking	4.4
Variety of merchandise in styles you like	4.4
Convenience of location relative to residence	4.1
Prices for quality offered	4.0

Source: ICSC Research

Table 2. How Lifestyle Centers Compare to Regional Centers on Eight Attributes

	Comparison to Regional Center		
	Better	Same	Worse
Overall atmosphere and shopping environment	65%	28%	5%
Convenience of parking	65%	25%	9%
Convenience of location relative to residence	58%	19%	22%
Feelings of safety and security	50%	47%	3%
Convenience of getting from store to store	43%	41%	14%
Quality of merchandise	28%	67%	3%
Variety of merchandise in styles you like	26%	45%	27%
Prices for quality offered	19%	68%	11%

Source: ICSC Research

Shopper Demographics

The median age of shoppers over age 18 at the five centers was 39.6. However, the variance across the centers was substantial, ranging from 33.6 to 43.1.

The age distribution of lifestyle center shoppers appeared to be slightly less weighted toward the younger and older age groups than regional malls. The lower proportion of lifestyle center customers vis-à-vis regional malls in the youngest age category probably reflected the smaller representation of teen retailers at lifestyle centers. **(See Figure 10.)**

Shoppers at these lifestyle centers were particularly affluent: median household income was almost $85,000, with a range from $63,200 to $107,100. Over half (57%) of the shoppers had household incomes above $75,000. These figures are particularly impressive when compared to the U.S. as a whole, where the median household income was $44,500 and 24% of households had incomes over $75,000. **Figure 11** graphically illustrates the high-income concentration of lifestyle center patrons.

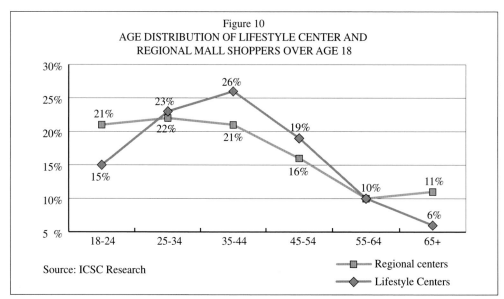

Figure 10
AGE DISTRIBUTION OF LIFESTYLE CENTER AND REGIONAL MALL SHOPPERS OVER AGE 18

Source: ICSC Research

These indices measure the degree to which the income profile of lifestyle center shoppers differs from that of the trade area they come from. For example, a score of 100 for a specific income group at a center means that this group is present in the center in the same proportion as in the center's trade area. A score in excess of 100 means that the group is over represented in the center.

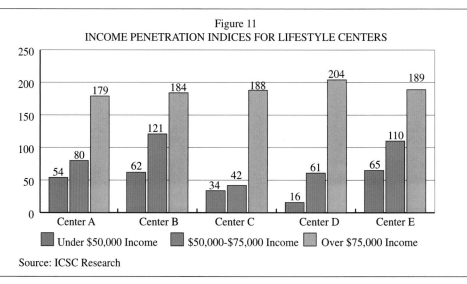

Figure 11
INCOME PENETRATION INDICES FOR LIFESTYLE CENTERS

Source: ICSC Research

Trade Area Definition

The trade areas (which accounted for an average of 74% of customers) for the five lifestyle centers ranged from relatively compact to very large, but tended to be quite large. The average number of ZIP codes encompassed by the five centers was 18. The population of the trade areas ranged from approximately 246,000 to 768,000, with a five-center average of nearly one-half million. The core trade areas, representing 53% of customers, had an average population of 201,000.

Mirroring the affluent profile of lifestyle center customers, their trading areas were also generally quite affluent: average household income among all the trading areas was $72,288, nearly one-fourth higher than the overall U.S. average. Approximately one-third of the core area (33%) and total trade area (30%) households had incomes of $75,000 or more. Average incomes were slightly higher in the core area ($76,982) than in the trade area as a whole ($72,288). **(See table 3.)**

As shown in **Figure 8,** core trade area residents visited the lifestyle centers more frequently than those in the balance of the trade area and those living outside the trade area. Core trade area residents were, not surprisingly, most likely to rate the centers as more "convenient" than their favorite regional mall.

Table 3. Summary Data From ICSC-Sponsored Interviews at Five Lifestyle Centers

	Center A	Center B	Center C	Center D	Center E	Average*
Trading Area Characteristics						
Number of ZIP Codes	30	26	5	14	13	18
Percent of Customers Interviewed	72%	72%	81%	72%	72%	74%
Population 1990	543,811	377,883	195,766	379,719	315,935	362,623
Population 2002	768,035	562,828	246,441	437,199	423,508	487,602
Population Change 1990-2002	224,224	184,945	50,675	57,480	107,573	124,979
Population Growth Rate 1990-2002	41.2%	48.9%	25.9%	15.1%	34.0%	34.5%
Number of Households 2002	295,913	232,666	92,116	162,480	171,524	190,940
Average Household Income 2002	$66,167	$57,154	$98,604	$101,156	$61,899	$72,288
No. of Households With Incomes $75,000+	94,132	52,216	38,219	63,849	36,978	57,079
Percent of Total Households With Incomes $75,000+	31.8%	22.4%	41.5%	39.3%	21.6%	29.9%
Core Area Characteristics						
Number of ZIP Codes	12	11	2	5	4	7
Percent of Customers Interviewed	56%	52%	51%	54%	53%	53%
Population 1990	217,809	166,946	81,934	138,225	106,200	142,223
Population 2002	343,084	247,741	95,251	173,152	147,230	201,292
Population Change 1990-2002	125,275	80,795	13,317	34,927	41,030	59,069
Population Growth Rate 1990-2002	57.5%	48.4%	16.3%	25.3%	38.6%	41.5%
Number of Households 2002	130,082	108,008	34,924	59,506	62,567	79,017
Average Household Income 2002	$69,318	$61,269	$106,302	$125,445	$57,584	$76,982
No. of Households With Incomes $75,000+	46,937	25,890	15,957	29,387	12,728	26,180
Percent of Total Households With Incomes $75,000+	36.1%	24.0%	45.7%	49.4%	20.3%	33.1%

(Averages are arithmetic, except for average household income and percent of total households with incomes $75,000+, which are weighted.)

Source: ICSC Research

Lifestyle Centers: The Big Picture

As evident from these five representative lifestyle centers, they are located in affluent trading areas and serve a largely affluent customer base.

The trade areas are also relatively large (averaging 18 ZIP codes as noted above), which is presumably the result of the uniqueness of the centers and the shopping experiences that are offered. The large trade areas are particularly impressive given that the lifestyle centers often have one-third or less the retail square footage of most regional shopping centers.

Despite the relatively large trade area draw of lifestyle centers, convenience is an important factor in their patronage patterns. Over half their customers live in the core part of the trading area most proximate to the lifestyle center and they patronize it on a frequent basis. Their customers also appreciate the convenience of the parking arrangements in comparison to regional malls.

In addition to matters of convenience, lifestyle center shoppers also endorse the overall atmosphere and shopping environment at these open-air facilities and feel safe and secure while shopping there.

Some of the basic characteristics of the lifestyle center shopper's trip are similar to those for regional shopping centers, such as the number of trips, the number of stores at which purchases are made and total expenditures. However, there is one notable difference—lifestyle center shoppers are more purpose-driven and the average trip duration to lifestyle centers is accordingly much shorter than for malls, at 57 minutes versus 78 minutes for a mall visit. Thus, given similar *per-trip* expenditure levels for lifestyle centers and malls, the lifestyle center trip yields more spending *per shopper hour*. This sense of efficiency surrounding the lifestyle center trip is bolstered by the attitudinal responses, in which the lifestyle center shoppers gave relatively high marks for convenience of parking and convenience of getting from store to store.

Finally, sales productivity at the four lifestyle centers, at an average of $325 psf (including anchors), compares favorably with that for regional malls ($336 psf of inline small tenant space in 2001 according to ICSC's *Monthly Merchandise Mall Index*).

Lifestyle centers appear to have established a viable niche in the pantheon of shopping center types. If they are well-located within affluent trading areas, well-executed and offer the proper tenant mix, they can attract shoppers with similar behaviors and spending patterns as regional malls.

Lifestyle centers cater particularly to the lifestyles of affluent shoppers. Developers of the centers strive to integrate them into their neighborhoods in keeping with the community's concern for grace, style, convenience and safety. The architectural features typically include fountains, lush landscaping, pedestrian-friendly courtyards, quality finishes with brick walls and decorated sidewalks with pavers, all in a "town center" environment. Restaurants are often an important part of the tenant mix and many use outdoor café seating for casual dining. To add to the entertainment offering, multi-screen movie theaters are frequently present. Specialty retailers offer casual apparel, housewares and home furnishings. Premier tenants include Chico's, Pottery Barn, Williams-Sonoma, Ann Taylor, Coldwater Creek, J. Jill, Banana Republic, Talbots and other retailers catering to the affluent suburban lifestyles of Americans in their mid-thirties and forties. Gourmet food stores are sometimes found in lifestyle centers, but rarely the big-box discounters and large supermarkets.

The lifestyle center is not necessarily a direct competitor with regional malls and trips to the two types of centers are often complementary: the lifestyle center for its convenience, efficiency and ambience; and the regional mall for its broader merchandise assortments and department store offering. As evident from ICSC research studies, for example, shoppers at the lifestyle center patronized it an average of 3.8 times a month, but also shopped their favorite regional mall an average of 2.5 times.

Section IV

Retailer Profiles

Abercrombie & Fitch

Kids and young adults have a great sense of loyalty to the Abercrombie brand.

A past that includes outfitting Ernest Hemingway and Theodore Roosevelt for safaries, this old-century-named retailer—Abercrombie & Fitch—outfits today's young adults, children, men and women.

Abercrombie & Fitch Co. is a leading specialty retailer encompassing three concepts: Abercrombie & Fitch; Abercrombie Kids; and Hollister Co. The company focuses on providing high-quality merchandise that complements the casual, classic American lifestyle.

Abercrombie & Fitch targets shoppers from 18 years old through college age, while Abercrombie Kids targets the 7 to 14 year old. The newest concept, launched in July 2000, is aimed at males and females 14 to 18 years old. Success within this demographic sector continues to be fueled, as young consumers appear to have a great sense of loyalty to the Abercrombie brand. Kids and young adults across the United States can be seen on campus—from junior-high school to college—wearing fashions with the Abercrombie logo.

Parent Company:	Abercrombie & Fitch Co.
Corporate Retail Headquarters:	6301 Fitch Path New Albany, OH 43054 (614) 283-6500 (614) 283-6710 Fax http://www.abercrombie.com

Annual Revenue:	$1.5 billion (2002)
# of U.S. States with Locations:	490 stores nationwide
U.S. Regions with Locations:	All
Locations Outside U.S.:	None

There are 490 stores throughout the United States.

The merchandise is sold in retail stores throughout the United States in approximately 490 mall stores and through catalogs. The company operates an e-commerce Web site at www.abercrombie.com and a kid's Web site at www.abercrombiekids.com, and it publishes a "magalog" called the *A&F Quarterly*.

Abercrombie & Fitch went public in 1996, and it spun off from The Limited in May 1998. The company reported a net sales increase of 17 percent last year, to $1.516 billion from $1.301 billion.

AMC Theatres

*A*MC is one of the biggest and most popular movie theatre companies in the world.

Parent Company:	AMC Entertainment, Inc.
Corporate Retail Headquarters:	920 Main Street Kansas City, MO 64105 (816) 221-4000 (816) 480-4617 Fax http://www.amctheatres.com

Annual Revenue:	$1,341.5 million
# of U.S. States with Locations:	250 multiplex and megaplex theatres in 29 states plus the District of Columbia
U.S. Regions with Locations:	All
Locations Outside U.S.:	Canada, France, Hong Kong, Japan, Portugal, Spain, Sweden, U.K.

In the year 2000, AMC Theatres celebrated 80 years of legacy and leadership, including its 1995 introduction of the megaplex concept to the United States with the opening of The Grand 24 in Dallas. This new concept established stadium-style seating and top-of-the-line amenities as the standard to which all theatres now aspire.

Wherever you look at movie history, AMC Entertainment, Inc. is there making an impact in the world of moviegoers. With innovations such as the first cup-holder armrests, automated tickets and the multitheatre megaplex, AMC has not only become a trendsetter but one of the most successful movie companies in history.

AMC Theatres continues to change the way people watch movies by transforming the experience into an adventure. The well-received stadium-style seating and state-of-the-art sound systems are just a few examples of its continued innovation as it further evolves the concept of the megaplex. Today, over 60 percent of AMC Theatres are megaplexes, containing at least 14 different movie screens.

With over 2,700 screens around the globe, AMC is already one of the biggest and most popular movie theatre companies in the world.

In addition to theatres in the United States, AMC can be found in Canada, France and Hong Kong, among other countries.

Ann Taylor

ANNTAYLOR

*A*nn Taylor sells *quality women's suits, separates, dresses, shoes and accessories.*

A full range of career, casual and occasion clothes and accessories are featured in each store.

Parent Company:	Ann Taylor Stores Corporation
Corporate Retail Headquarters:	142 W. 57th Street New York, NY 10019 (212) 541-3300 (212) 541-3379 Fax http://www.anntaylor.com
Annual Revenue (for Ann Taylor Stores Corporation):	$352.2 million (2002)
# of U.S. States with Locations:	351 Ann Taylor, 207 Ann Taylor Loft and 27 Ann Taylor Factory Stores in 42 states plus the District of Columbia and Puerto Rico
U.S. Regions with Locations:	All
Locations Outside U.S.:	None

Many people continue to ask, "Is there a real Ann Taylor?" The answer: Ann Taylor was the name of a best-selling dress at the founder's father's store. Both the best-selling dress and the name Ann Taylor were passed from father to son for good luck. The first Ann Taylor store opened in New Haven, Connecticut, in 1954, and, since then, there has been much more than just luck.

Ann Taylor is a premier American specialty-apparel retailer for the professional woman. Over the company's 47-year heritage, it has become a well-known resource for quality suits, separates, dresses, shoes and accessories, with a feminine, polished approach to updated classic styles. The company meets the needs of modern women's busy lifestyles by providing a full range of career, casual and occasion offerings in one location.

The brand is marketed under two divisions, Ann Taylor and Ann Taylor Loft. The company's Ann Taylor stores compete in the "better-priced" category and cater to the successful, relatively affluent career woman, who needs appropriate, fashion-conscious attire for her professional life and prefers stylish, coordinated looks for her leisure activities.

Ann Taylor Loft stores compete in the "upper-moderate-priced" category. Ann Taylor Loft collections are designed for women with a more relaxed lifestyle both at work and at home who appreciate the Ann Taylor brand but are unwilling to pay Ann Taylor-store prices.

*F*ounded in 1954, Ann Taylor continues its legacy as a premier American specialty-retailer serving the modern woman.

Anthropologie

There are 40 Anthropologie stores in 19 states in the United States.

Anthropologie is true to its culture and the significance of its name: A study of foreign cultures that brings richness and meaning. This is embodied in the feel of the store, from its displays and architecture to its merchandise. A simple cup in a Dutch farmhouse, a bolt of richly embroidered fabric in an Indian dress shop — these objects and icons of everyday life in other countries become the beautiful works of art at Anthropologie. Its products include women's apparel, accessories, home décor and gifts. Anthropologie operates 40 stores in 19 states.

*M*erchandise featured includes women's apparel, accessories, home décor and gifts.

Parent Company:	Anthropologie LLC, a subsidiary of Urban Outfitters, Inc.
Corporate Retail Headquarters:	1809 Walnut Street Philadelphia, PA 19103 (215) 564-2313 (215) 568-1549 Fax http://www.anthropologie.com

Annual Revenue (for Urban Outfitters, Inc.):	$422.8 million (2003)
# of U.S. States with Locations:	40 stores in 19 states
U.S. Regions with Locations:	All
Locations Outside U.S.:	None

*D*isplays and architecture embody the feel of the store.

Apple Store

   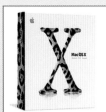

There are currently over 50 Apple Stores in the United States.

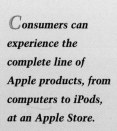

Consumers can experience the complete line of Apple products, from computers to iPods, at an Apple Store.

Parent Company:	Apple Computer, Inc.
Corporate Retail Headquarters:	1 Infinite Loop Cupertino, CA 9504 (408) 996-1010 (408) 974-2113 Fax http://www.apple.com

# of U.S. States with Locations:	58 stores in 26 states
U.S. Regions with Locations:	All
Locations Outside U.S.:	None

At an Apple Store, consumers can experience the complete line of Macintosh computers and an amazing array of digital cameras, camcorders, the entire iPod family and much more in a very inviting atmosphere.

The interactive Apple Store is a place to ask questions and get answers. And it's the best place to learn about the "Mac." There is plenty of staff on hand eager to help customers discover the "Mac" that's right for them.

Consumers can fully experience the digital lifestyle on a "Mac" at one of Apple's own retail stores. The "try-before-you-buy" approach continues to prove well for both the retailer and the consumer. There are currently over 50 stores in approximately 25 states across the United States.

An Apple Store is a good place to learn about Apple products, including the Macintosh computer.

Aveda

Aveda takes its cosmetic products to consumers through "environmental lifestyle" stores, salons and spas.

Parent Company:	The Estée Lauder Companies, Inc.
Corporate Retail Headquarters:	767 5th Avenue New York, NY 10153 (212) 572-4200 (212) 572-6633 http://www.elcompanies.com
Annual Revenue (for The Estée Lauder Companies, Inc.):	$4.7 billion (2002)
# of U.S. States with Locations:	50 states plus the District of Columbia and Puerto Rico
U.S. Regions with Locations:	All
Locations Outside U.S.:	Australia, Austria, Belgium, Bermuda, Canada, France, Germany, Hong Kong, Iceland, Ireland, Italy, Korea, Malaysia, Netherlands, New Zealand, Switzerland, Taiwan, U.K.

Aveda takes its cosmetic products to its consumers through a wide network of "environmental lifestyle" stores, salons and spas. It offers caffeine-free herbal tea, Pure-Fumes™ fragrances, stress-relieving massages, skin care products and consultations, makeup and hair care products and styling. Its products stress today's modern consumer's sense of responsibility about the environment and biodiversity. Aveda also promotes aroma therapy, yoga, meditation and time spent with nature.

The company has stores in 50 states plus the District of Columbia and Puerto Rico.

Among the products and services offered are skin care products and consultations, massages and makeup and hair care products.

Bahama Breeze

Reflecting the culinary diversity of the Caribbean, Bahama Breeze prepares a wide range of seafood, meat, chicken and pasta dishes, among others.

Bahama Breeze℠ take the tour!

the greatest culinary crossroads in the world with all the bold and unique flavors of the Caribbean!

Bahama Breeze restaurants operate in 16 states.

Parent Company:	Darden Restaurants
Corporate Retail Headquarters:	5900 Lake Ellenor Drive Orlando, FL 32809 (407) 245-2563 (407) 245-4462 Fax http://www.bahamabreeze.com

Annual Revenue (for Darden Restaurants):	$4.4 billion (2002)
Typical Store/Location Size:	7,000 to 10,000 square feet
# of U.S. States with Locations:	16 states
U.S. Regions with Locations:	All
Locations Outside U.S.:	None

A visit to Bahama Breeze is like a mini-vacation to a Caribbean island, complete with bold flavors, colorful sights, tropical drinks, live music and happy, upbeat people. Reflecting the culinary diversity of the Caribbean, Bahama Breeze prepares a wide range of seafood and pasta dishes, beef, pork and chicken items and even pizzas. An open kitchen where the cooking is on display creates an exciting atmosphere and anticipation that raises diners' expectations. This is the heart of Bahama Breeze.

This new, vibrant business has been setting and resetting sales records at each of its restaurants since opening.

Bahama Breeze is the freshest, most exciting restaurant concept to hit the restaurant industry in years. Great food is the heart of the concept and it is magnified by excellent service and an energetic atmosphere. Operated by Darden Restaurants, sister companies include Red Lobster and Olive Garden, among others.

Great Caribbean food, freshly prepared in unique and delightful ways, is a great excuse to pay a visit to Bahama Breeze. From the unique appetizers and the remarkable entrées to the artfully presented and sumptuous desserts, diners experience a meal that is unlike any other.

Banana Republic

*S*election, versatility and quality are key at Banana Republic.

Parent Company:	The Gap, Inc.
Corporate Retail Headquarters:	2 Folsom Street San Francisco, CA 94105 (650) 952-4400 (415) 427-2553 Fax http://www.gap.com
Annual Revenue (for the Gap, Inc.):	$14.4 billion (2002)
# of U.S. States with Locations:	All (4,300 stores worldwide)
U.S. Regions with Locations:	All
Locations Outside U.S.:	Canada, France, Japan, Germany, United Kingdom

A division of The Gap, Inc., Banana Republic is known for casual luxury, with high-quality apparel for men and women and sophisticated seasonal collections of accessories, shoes, personal-care products, intimate apparel and gifts for the home. It has become known as the location for products that are modern, versatile and of exceptional quality. Banana Republic customers love fashion—fashion from a point of view that is sophisticated, yet relaxed and easy—and it offers the right wardrobe for any occasion.

Banana Republic keeps their look modern.

Barnes & Noble Booksellers

Barnes & Noble is the largest bookseller in the United States, with over 620 stores.

At the heart of Barnes & Noble is the store experience.

The company's founder and current Chairman, Leonard Riggio, saw bookstores as community centers, places where people could be and become. Everything Barnes & Noble does, from the design of its stores and the selection of its titles to the training of its booksellers, reflects that philosophy.

Barnes & Noble believes that a great bookstore does more than just sell books. Customers are welcome to browse, read, chat, think, debate or simply relax with a cup of coffee in one of over 620 superstores located across the country.

As the nation's largest bookseller, there are approximately 900 stores in 49 states and the District of Columbia under the Barnes & Noble and B. Dalton names.

Parent Company:	Barnes & Noble, Inc.
Corporate Retail Headquarters:	122 Fifth Avenue New York, NY 10011 (212) 633-3300 (212) 675-0413 Fax http://www.barnesandnoble.com

Annual Revenue:	$5.3 billion
# of U.S. States with Locations:	620 Barnes & Noble stores in 49 states plus the District of Columbia
U.S. Regions with Locations:	All
Locations Outside U.S.:	None

*C*ustomers are welcome to browse, read and relax over a cup of coffee in Barnes & Noble stores.

*S*tores can be found in 49 states plus the District of Columbia in the United States.

Big Bowl Asian Kitchen

Big Bowl Asian Kitchen features Asian-inspired dishes prepared in an open-display kitchen.

Big Bowl Asian Kitchen provides a fresh approach to Asian cooking. A casual neighborhood restaurant, it features Asian-inspired dishes prepared fresh in an open display kitchen. Offering an array of appetizers such as chicken pot stickers, Thai herb calamari and distinctive entrées, the restaurant prepares delicious contemporary versions of traditional Asian dishes such as spicy kung pao, pad thai and crispy lemon chicken.

The stir-fry bar allows guests to help themselves to fresh vegetables that are then cooked to order with the diner's choice of sauces and

Parent Company:	Brinker International
Corporate Retail Headquarters:	6820 LBJ Freeway Dallas, TX 75240 (972) 980-9917 http://www.bigbowl.com
Annual Revenue (for Brinker International):	$3 billion
Typical Store/Location Size:	5,500 square feet (varies widely)
# of U.S. States with Locations:	18 locations in 6 states (Illinois, Texas, Colorado, Minnesota, North Carolina, Virginia)
U.S. Regions with Locations:	Central/Midwest, Southern
Locations Outside U.S.:	None

meats and served with noodles or rice. This colorful and interactive centerpiece provides a healthy option and great value to guests. Big Bowl Asian Kitchen offers distinctive nonalcoholic beverages such as homemade ginger ale and Japanese-style hot tea service. There is also a full-service bar, serving signature cocktails such as frozen mai tais and golden Buddha margaritas.

Big Bowl Asian Kitchen offers an award-winning children's menu that includes a free bowl of rice and a packet filled with toys and games when the children are seated. The restaurant offers a "group share" option for parties of six or more, giving groups an affordable way to share appetizers and entrées. Most locations have a separate area available for private parties. Big Bowl Asian Kitchen appeals to all ages, from kids to connoisseurs. It offers value for every occasion, whether it be dining in, taking out or accommodating a large group of diners, with most entrees under $10. Big Bowl Asian Kitchen operates 18 restaurants in six states.

Blue Mesa Grill

*O*pen daily for lunch and dinner and Sunday brunch, the restaurant can accommodate events and private parties for all occasions.

*B*lue Mesa Grill delivers the bold, colorful tastes of the Southwest, with an emphasis on mesquite grilling, fresh ingredients and one-of-a-kind recipes. Signature items include tableside guacamole, red-chili-crusted salmon, smoky Texas rib-eye steak and Churrascaritas™, richly flavored skewers of meats and vegetables served with grilled bread. Abundant and colorful plate presentations at moderate prices translate into great value.

Blue Mesa also accommodates events and private parties for all types of occasions, including weddings, rehearsal dinners, showers, office parties, business

*B*lue Mesa Grill emphasizes mesquite grilling, fresh ingredients and one-of-a-kind recipes.

Currently located in Texas only, Blue Mesa operates 5 restaurants.

Parent Company:	Mesa SW Restaurants, Inc.
Corporate Retail Headquarters:	6540 Forest Creek Drive Dallas, TX 75230 (214) 891-9989 (214) 363-6783 Fax http://www.bluemesagrill.com
Annual Revenue:	$13 million
Typical Store/Location Size:	7,500 square feet
# of U.S. States with Locations:	5 restaurants in 1 state (Texas)
U.S. Regions with Locations:	Central
Locations Outside U.S.:	None

lunches and other get-togethers. Catering, including box lunches, is also available.

Blue Mesa has been recognized in Texas' Dallas-Fort Worth *Zagat Survey* as one of the top Southwestern restaurants. It is open daily for lunch and dinner and offers a happy hour from Monday to Friday. It is famous for its legendary Sunday brunch, which has been named "Best Sunday Brunch" for several years by the *Dallas Observer*.

Blue Mesa restaurants, which are currently located in Texas only, requires 7,500 square feet.

BLUE MESA CAFÉ

The Bombay Company

Bombay features classic and traditional furniture as well as coordinating accessories and wall décor.

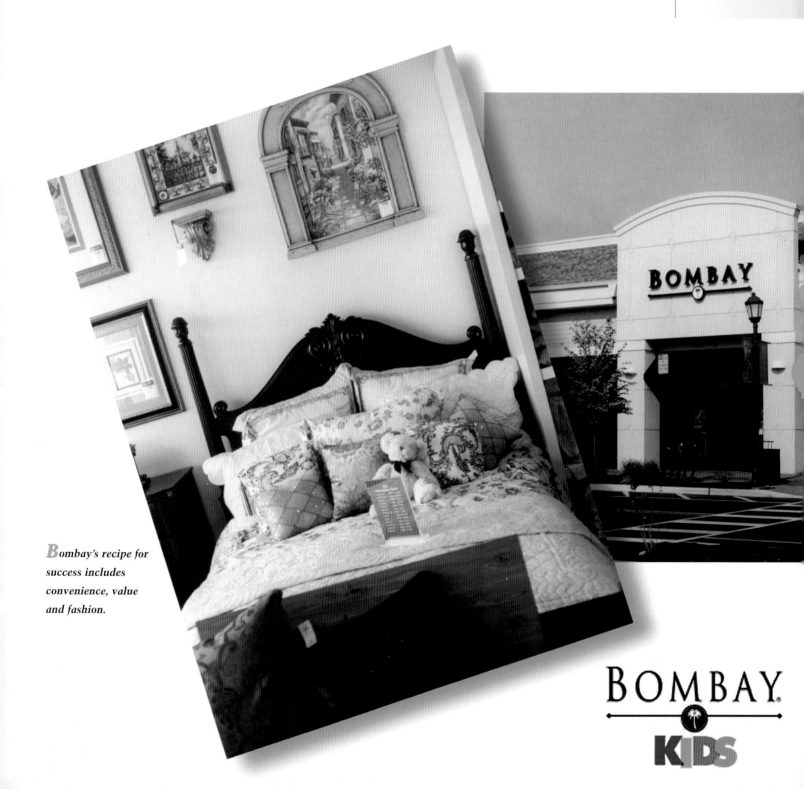

Bombay's recipe for success includes convenience, value and fashion.

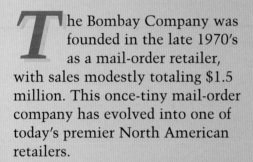

Parent Company:	The Bombay Company, Inc.
Corporate Retail Headquarters:	550 Bailey Avenue Fort Worth, TX 76107 (817) 347-8200 (817) 332-7066 Fax http://www.bombayco.com
Annual Revenue:	$437.5 million (2002)
Typical Store/Location Size:	Combination stores: 8,500 to 9,000 square feet; large format: 4,500 square feet; BombayKIDS: 4,000 square feet; outlets: 4,500 square feet; regular: 1,800 square feet
# of U.S. States with Locations:	420 stores in most states plus the District of Columbia
U.S. Regions with Locations:	All
Locations Outside U.S.:	Canada

The Bombay Company was founded in the late 1970's as a mail-order retailer, with sales modestly totaling $1.5 million. This once-tiny mail-order company has evolved into one of today's premier North American retailers.

Tandy Brands eventually purchased the company, believing that the ready-to-assemble furniture concept was a potential retail store home run. It opened the first two stores in 1980, followed by a handful of additional stores to test various markets. At the same time, a Canadian, Robert Nourse, purchased the rights to develop The Bombay Company in Canada, and he opened his first store in April 1980.

In late 1983, Tandy Brands merged the United States and Canadian operations under Mr. Nourse. Bombay's recipe for success was convenience, value and fashion. Customers rapidly adopted the concept due to its fashionable products—ones they could take home with them.

The style and tone of Bombay reflects a sophisticated look and features classic and traditional furniture as well as coordinating accessories and wall décor. Staying current with customers' needs and everyday lifestyle changes, Bombay now offers complete collections focused on the rooms that are most relevant to the customer—the home office, bedroom, dining room and family room.

At the end of 2002, The Bombay Company, which includes Bombay Kids, had annual revenues of over $437.5 million and 420 stores in the United States and Canada.

Borders Superstores

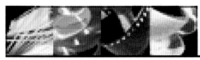 BORDERS®

Borders is a leading global retailer of books, music, movies and other information and entertainment items.

INSIDE
BORDERS

Parent Company:	Borders Group, Inc.
Corporate Retail Headquarters:	100 Phoenix Drive Ann Arbor, MI 48108 http://bordersgroupinc.com
Annual Revenue (for Borders Group, Inc.):	$3.51 billion
# of U.S. States with Locations:	435 superstores in 50 states plus the District of Columbia and Puerto Rico
Locations Outside U.S.:	U.K., Australia, New Zealand, Singapore

Borders Group, Inc. is a leading global retailer of books, music, movies and other information and entertainment items. Headquartered in Ann Arbor, Michigan, Borders Group operates 435 Borders Books and Music stores in the United States as well as 29 international Borders stores, approximately 800 Waldenbooks locations and 37 Books etc. stores in the United Kingdom. Online shopping is available at each store's Web site, which has been teamed with Amazon.com.

Borders stores offer the community a comfortable place to explore over 140,000 book, music, DVD and periodical titles as well as the opportunity to experience cutting-edge service technology backed by a knowledgeable staff with a commitment to the community. Free events such as lectures, author signings, musical performances, children's activities and "Benefit Days" that support local charities are held throughout the year.

As a retailer, Borders is unique in tailoring its title base to respond to the interests of the customers who shop at each store location. Just 50 percent of Borders' title base is common to all stores, while the other half is customized to the location by experienced buyers using the company's sophisticated computerized inventory system.

In addition to offering books, music and movies, Borders invites shoppers to unwind at Café Borders. Customers of the café can choose from a variety of gourmet coffees, teas and beverages and enjoy desserts and light snack items.

Brookstone

Brookstone offers a unique line of consumer products not widely available from other retailers in a fun, interactive shopping environment.

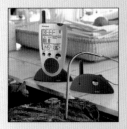

Parent Company:	Brookstone, Inc.
Corporate Retail Headquarters:	17 Riverside Street Nashua, NH 03062 (603) 880-9500 (603) 577-8004 Fax http://www.brookstone.com

Annual Revenue:	$375.9 million
# of U.S. States with Locations:	258 stores in 39 states plus the District of Columbia and Puerto Rico
U.S. Regions with Locations:	All
Locations Outside U.S.:	None

Brookstone

Brookstone is a nationwide specialty retailer offering an assortment of consumer products that are functional in purpose, distinctive in quality and design and not widely available from other retailers. Brookstone first introduced itself to the world in a small classified ad selling "hard-to-find tools" in *Popular Mechanics* magazine. The year was 1965.

From the beginning, quality of product, quality of service and quality of people have been a hallmark of Brookstone. The first catalog consisted of 24 black-and-white pages, with detailed, no-nonsense information on features, capabilities, measurements, materials and anything that would help customers with their buying decisions.

As Brookstone's catalog success grew, its operations expanded. In 1973, Brookstone opened its first retail store in Peterborough, New

Hampshire. Today, Brookstone's headquarters is located in Nashua, New Hampshire. There are 258 retail stores (with more planned) in the United States from coast to coast. Annual sales are $375.9 million.

From the start, Brookstone wanted to create a fun, interactive shopping experience. At its stores, customers are encouraged to try products out for true, hands-on shopping. Every visit to Brookstone is an opportunity to discover new and ingenious items of superior quality—all in a friendly environment of customer service and integrity that simply can't be found anywhere else.

The consistently unique line of products, the fun interactive shopping environment and the detailed catalogs are the reason more and more people seek out Brookstone each year.

California Pizza Kitchen

*H*earth-baked pizzas are served at California Pizza Kitchens in 26 states plus the District of Columbia and several foreign countries.

*P*astas, salads, soups and sides are among the menu options in addition to pizzas.

California Pizza Kitchen introduces flavors and tastes from around the world, from Thai to tandoori, all on a pizza.

Parent Company:	California Pizza Kitchen, Inc.
Corporate Retail Headquarters:	6053 W. Century Boulevard Los Angeles, CA 90045 (310) 342-5000 (310) 342-4743 Fax http://www.cpk.com

Annual Revenue:	$303 million (2002)
Typical Store/Location Size:	5,000 square feet
# of U.S. States with Locations:	122 CPK plus 24 CPK/ASAP restaurants in 26 states and the District of Columbia
U.S. Regions with Locations:	All
Locations Outside U.S.:	9 international locations in Indonesia, Malaysia, Philippines, Singapore

*I*n 1985, attorneys Rick Rosenfield and Larry Flax traded in the courtroom for the dining room. Having always wanted to get into the restaurant business, they pitched their legal pads to serve hearth-baked pizzas and created California Pizza Kitchen (CPK).

They introduced flavors and tastes from around the world, from Thai to tandoori, all on a pizza, and created the original BBQ chicken pizza. Pizza lovers were jolted out of the traditional pepperoni pizzas and introduced to pizzas such as BLT bliss, Thai chicken euphoria and tandoori chicken nirvana. Not limiting their menu to just pizza, they created an innovative selection of pastas, salads and desserts.

Now, California Pizza Kitchen is a leading casual-dining chain in the premium-pizza segment, with a recognized consumer brand and an established, loyal customer base. There are currently over 120 full-service restaurants in over 26 states, the District of Columbia and four foreign countries.

CPK has a strong brand awareness and recently developed a high-quality, quick-service, casual-dining concept called CPK/ASAP. The CPK/ASAP restaurants are significantly smaller than the full-service restaurants and offer a limited selection of only the most popular pizzas, salads, sandwiches and appetizers. There currently are over 24 CPK/ASAP locations throughout the United States.

The Cheesecake Factory

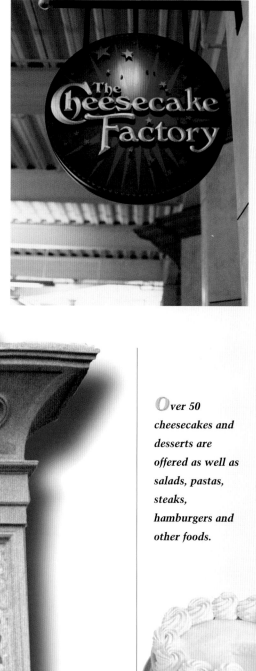

*D*istinctive architecture and stylish décor add to the dining experience at The Cheesecake Factory.

*O*ver 50 cheesecakes and desserts are offered as well as salads, pastas, steaks, hamburgers and other foods.

Parent Company:	The Cheesecake Factory, Inc.
Corporate Retail Headquarters:	26950 Agoura Road Calabasas Hills, CA 91301 (818) 871-3000 (818) 871-3100 Fax http://www.thecheesecakefactory.com
Annual Revenue:	$652.0 million (2002)
Typical Store/Location Size:	5,400 to 17,300 square feet
# of U.S. States with Locations:	60 restaurants in 22 states
U.S. Regions with Locations:	All
Locations Outside U.S.:	None

The company originated in 1972 as a producer and distributor of high-quality cheesecakes and other baked desserts. The first restaurant opened in Beverly Hills, California, in 1978.

Distinctive architecture, stylish décor, superior service and an extensive, innovative menu with generous portions at moderate prices combine to create an overall dining experience with unparalleled value.

The Cheesecake Factory is a high-energy atmosphere seven days a week, serving lunch, dinner, late-night supper, beverages from a full bar, Sunday brunch and take-out food. An extensive menu offers diners over 200 selections from avocado egg rolls, Chinese chicken salad, pasta, specialty pizza, sandwiches, steaks, fresh fish and omelette's to classic hamburgers and over 50 delicious cheesecakes and desserts. Full-service Cheesecake Factory restaurants currently range in size from 5,400 to 17,300 interior square feet.

There are 60 Cheesecake Factory restaurants across the country. Grand Lux Cafe®, the company's upscale casual-dining restaurant created for the Venetian Resort-Hotel-Casino in Las Vegas, Nevada, was opened in May 1999.

The creation, production and marketing of quality cheesecakes and other baked desserts remain a cornerstone of the company's brand identity.

The Cheesecake Factory operates seven days a week, serving lunch, dinner, late-night supper, Sunday brunch and take-out food and beverages.

Chico's

CHICO'S

There are 138 stores and 74 factory-outlet stores in the United States, with two stores in the United Kingdom.

This is indeed a fashion company cut from a different cloth. Established in 1983, Chico's began as a small store on Sanibel Island, Florida, with Marvin and Helene Gralnick selling Mexican folk art and cotton sweaters. Now, 19 years later, Chico's has grown to over 360 stores nationwide.

From exclusive, private-label designs to amazing personal service, Chico's is truly a unique retail environment. When customers walk into any Chico's store, they can depend upon the sales staff to coordinate, accessorize and help them build a wardrobe to suit their needs. All products are designed and developed by the in-house product development team at Chico's headquarters in Fort Myers, Florida.

The private-label brand specializes in sophisticated casual to dressy clothing, complementary accessories and other nonclothing gift items all bearing the Chico's trademark look. The boutiques target middle- to high-income women ages 35 to 65 years old and offer them color-coordinated clothes made primarily from natural fabrics such as cotton, linen and silk. New styles are provided every week, keeping the customer returning again and again. Plans are to introduce a new concept, Pazo, intended to target women 25 to 35 years old and to sell American and European fashions.

Parent Company:	Chico's FAS, Inc.
Corporate Retail Headquarters:	11215 Metro Parkway Fort Myers, FL 33912 (239) 277-6200 (239) 277-5237 Fax http://www.chicos.com

Annual Revenue:	$531 million (2002)
Typical Store/Location Size:	1,000 to 3,500 square feet
# of U.S. States with Locations:	406 Chico's and Chico's outlet stores in 41 states plus the District of Columbia
U.S. Regions with Locations:	All
Locations Outside U.S.:	None

Chico's started operations with one store in 1983, went public in March 1993 with 75 stores and, as of December 31, 2002, operated 406 stores in 41 states plus the District of Columbia, 12 of which were franchised (the company stopped all new franchising activities in 1989). Stores range in size from 1,000 to 3,500 square feet of selling space.

The majority of rapid growth occurred over the last few years. Customer loyalty, combined with national advertising and active e-commerce and catalog segments, enable a highly experienced retail team to soar at Chico's, which was originally named after a bilingual parrot owned by the founders' friends.

There are 406 Chico's stores and factory-outlet stores in the United States.

Chili's

Like No Place Else.

Chili's has 49 restaurants in the United States as well as locations in Canada, Mexico, the United Kingdom and Peru, among other countries.

Chili's traces its original roots to 1975, when the first Chili's opened with one restaurant on Greenville Avenue in Dallas. Chili's first started as a neighborhood-style restaurant that served quality homemade food in a casual atmosphere. Sales grew quickly and additional restaurants flourished.

Chili's growth exploded in the 1980's as a nation of hungry baby boomers satisfied their cravings for good food and good times. Today, the success continues with signature menu items like big

Parent Company:	Brinker International
Corporate Retail Headquarters:	6820 LBJ Freeway Dallas, TX 75240 (972) 980-9917 http://www.chilis.com
Annual Revenue (for Brinker International):	$3 billion
Typical Store/Location Size:	5,500 square feet (varies widely)
# of U.S. States with Locations:	49 plus Puerto Rico
U.S. Regions with Locations:	All
Locations Outside U.S.:	90 restaurants in 21 countries, including Canada, Mexico, several in the Middle East, U.K., Australia, Taiwan, Korea, Venezuela, Peru and others

mouth hamburgers, fajitas, baby back ribs, presidente margaritas and the popular guiltless grill menu.

Chili's quickly earned a reputation as a restaurant industry barometer, and it continues to set the pace for all other casual-dining restaurants.

Chili's is a casual-dining restaurant with signature items such as big mouth hamburgers, fajitas and baby back ribs, among other food and beverage items.

Coach

A wide variety of handbags, shoes and accessories are featured.

Coach designs, produces and sells classically styled, high-quality leather goods.

Parent Company:	Coach, Inc.
Corporate Retail Headquarters:	516 W. 34th Street New York, NY 10001 (212) 594-1850 (212) 594-1682 Fax http://www.coach.com
Annual Revenue:	$719.4 million (2002)
# of U.S. States with Locations:	138 stores and 74 factory stores in 50 states plus the District of Columbia and Puerto Rico
U.S. Regions with Locations:	All
Locations Outside U.S.:	2 stores in the U.K. and manufacturing in Italy and China. Sells wholesale to department stores, retail stores, factory stores and duty-free shops internationally. Through an affiliate operates 83 retail and department store locations in Japan.

Coach designs and produces classically styled, high-quality leather goods and accessories for men and women, including luggage, purses, outerwear and gloves.

Coach products are glove-tanned pieces crafted from natural leather that burnishes over time, acquiring a rich, lustrous patina. From handbags to backpacks, each style features signature details such as distinctive hardware, double-needle stitching and bound edges. The shapes soften gradually to the touch, taking on the individual imprint of the wearer.

The Business Collection features a broad range of pieces, including briefcases, organizers, planners, notepads, computer cases and cellphone cases. Function is paramount, as is an understated sophistication.

The Travel Collection is a luxurious assortment of highly durable and functional luggage and travel accessories in leather and lightweight travel twill created to address the diverse needs of business and weekend travelers. Beyond these collections, Coach offers a variety of handbags and accessories encompassing a wide range of materials and updated designs.

Founded in 1941, the company also licenses its name for watches, footwear and furniture. In addition to 138 stores and 74 factory-outlet Coach stores in the United States and two in the United Kingdom, Coach sells its wares through department stores in the United States and in 18 other countries, via catalogs and through its Web site. Current plans are to open approximately 20 new stores a year.

There are 138 stores and 74 factory-outlet stores in the United States, with two stores in the United Kingdom.

Coldwater Creek

Coldwater Creek specializes in casual clothing, accessories and gifts that carry the wide-open flavor of the Rocky Mountains.

Typical customers are women who are 35 to 60 years old.

Parent Company:	Coldwater Creek, Inc.
Corporate Retail Headquarters:	One Coldwater Creek Drive Sandpoint, ID 83864 (208) 263-2266 (208) 263-1582 Fax http://www.coldwatercreek.com

Annual Revenue:	$464 million
Typical Store/Location Size:	5,250 square feet
# of U.S. States with Locations:	43 stores in 30 states and planning to open 23 more stores in 2003
U.S. Regions with Locations:	All
Locations Outside U.S.:	None

Founded in 1984, Coldwater Creek began as a home business with only one phone with an extra-long cord, a closet stuffed with merchandise and a fierce determination to set new standards for mail-order service. Today, the employee roster has swelled to about 2,200 and the home office has grown to a 20-acre campus surrounded by broad Rocky Mountain vistas. Tucked away in the Rocky Mountains on the shores of Lake Pend Oreille, Coldwater Creek is headquartered in Sandpoint, Idaho.

The company was founded by Dennis and Ann Pence, who remain with Coldwater Creek as Chairman of the Board and Creative Director/Vice-Chairman respectively. The first catalog was an 18-page mailer distributed to a customer file of about 2,000 names. Coldwater Creek currently has a customer file of more than 10 million names, and, in 2001, it mailed more than 160 million catalogs.

Specializing in casual clothing, accessories and gifts that carry the wide-open flavor of the Rockies, Coldwater Creek's merchandise suits decidedly urban landscapes as well. Nature-inspired jewelry, some with echoes of Native America, and nature-related gifts delight as well as inform. Beautiful items for the home are also featured.

The Coldwater Creek customer profile is a professional woman, from 35 to 60 years of age, who puts in a long workweek before going home to care for her family. She is educated, has more discretionary income than free time and favors the ease of catalog and Internet shopping. When she does have time, however, she still prefers to "experience the brand" in the brick-and-mortar retail setting.

Coldwater Creek is therefore a multichannel retailer selling through its core catalogs, via its e-commerce Web site and through a growing number of highly visible retail stores located in major

Coldwater Creek sells its merchandise through catalogs, a Web site and a growing number of stores in major metropolitan areas.

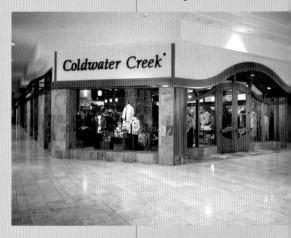

Parent Company:	J. Crew Group, Inc.
Corporate Retail Headquarters:	770 Broadway New York, NY 10003 (212) 209-2500 (212) 209-2666 Fax http://www.jcrew.com
Annual Revenue:	$777.9 million (2002)
# of U.S. States with Locations:	175 stores nationwide
U.S. Regions with Locations:	All
Locations Outside U.S.:	60 stores in Japan

Launched in 1996, jcrew.com, a Web site, allows customers to browse through pages of the catalog and place online orders. J. Crew became one of the first retailers to pioneer the transformation from traditional retailer to the world of e-commerce.

Already an $800 million brand, J. Crew continues to grow rapidly through an expanding retail store network, an industry-leading Web site and a famous catalog as it remains committed to exceeding the expectations of its customers.

J. Jill

J. Jill is a specialty retailer of high-quality women's apparel, accessories and footwear.

Merchandise ranges from relaxed career wear to weekend wear.

Parent Company:	The J. Jill Group, Inc.
Corporate Retail Headquarters:	4 Batterymarch Park Quincy, MA 02169 (617) 376-4300 (617) 769-0177 Fax http://www.jjill.com

Annual Revenue:	$347.6 million
# of U.S. States with Locations:	94 stores in 30 states
U.S. Regions with Locations:	All
Locations Outside U.S.:	None

The J. Jill Group, Inc. is a specialty retailer of high-quality women's apparel, accessories and footwear. The J. Jill brand is characterized by the simple, comfortable, versatile style of its merchandise offerings. Emphasizing natural fibers and unique details, J. Jill merchandise ranges from relaxed career wear to weekend wear. Almost all of the company's merchandise is private label (that is, sold under the J. Jill brand name). Many of the company's private-label offerings are designed by the company's product-development team and are not available in other catalogs or retail stores. J. Jill's targeted customers are active, affluent women who are 35 to 55 years old.

J. Jill markets its products through its catalogs, retail stores and Web site. During 1999, the company shifted from being a direct-mail retailer with a multiple-catalog concept to being a single-brand retailer with multiple distribution channels.

The company currently has two distinct business segments: Direct and retail. Both of these segments are focused on selling J. Jill merchandise. Each segment is separately managed and utilizes distinct distribution, marketing and inventory management strategies. The direct segment markets merchandise through catalogs and a Web site. The retail segment sells the same merchandise through retail stores.

The J. Jill brand is being built into a premier national brand through its multichannel distribution philosophy, as the combination of "mail, mall and Web" is the most powerful formula in specialty retailing today. The company believes it will reach a broader audience and be able to introduce the J. Jill brand to untapped markets. The mature woman is J. Jill's targeted customer. J. Jill is well-positioned to meet this customer's needs and, therefore, to capture an increased share of business in this underserved market.

The mature woman is J. Jill's targeted customer.

Maggiano's Little Italy

*I*n a vibrant atmosphere filled with the nostalgic Italian charm of red-checked table-cloths and family portraits, Maggiano's welcomes you to a warm and unique dining experience.

From the very beginning, at the first Maggiano's in 1991, and continuing today, Maggiano's blends the tradition of family, the celebration of friends and the cuisine of authentic Italy in an atmosphere often said to be reminiscent of pre-World War II Little Italy.

Maggiano's offers an enticing menu full of Old and New World southern Italian recipes, popular house specialties, irresistible desserts and a large selection of wines. The "made-from-scratch" menu items replicate everyday recipes that have been in Italian families for many, many years. The "varied" wine cellar boasts flavors from all over the world.

In the beautiful main dining room, there are tables for 2-14 diners and preset menus that offer "family-style dining," with "off-the-menu" options for diners to select from as well. For larger groups, elegant banquet rooms are available.

Maggiano's Little Italy is part of the Dallas-based Brinker International, one of the most influential, trendsetting, multiconcept operators in the restaurant industry, tracing its original roots to 1975.

*"**F**amily-style dining" in the main dining room and elegant banquet rooms for larger parties are among the dining options.*

Parent Company:	Brinker International
Corporate Retail Headquarters:	6820 LBJ Freeway Dallas, TX 75240 (972) 980-9917 http://www.maggianos.com
Annual Revenue (for Brinker International):	$3 billion
Typical Store/Location Size:	5,500 square feet (varies widely)
# of U.S. States with Locations:	18 states plus the District of Columbia
U.S. Regions with Locations:	All
Locations Outside U.S.:	None

***M**aggiano's Little Italy offers an enticing menu of southern Italian recipes, desserts and wines.*

Noodles & Company

Noodles & Company serves all kinds of noodles—from stir-fried noodles to macaroni and cheese.

There are 63 restaurants in nine states.

Parent Company:	Noodles & Company
Corporate Retail Headquarters:	2590 Pearl Street Boulder, CO 80302 (720) 214-1900 (720) 214-1934 Fax http://www.noodles.com

Annual Revenue:	$80 million (2003)
Typical Store/Location Size:	2,500 square feet
# of U.S. States with Locations:	63 restaurants in 9 states (Minnesota, Illinois, Colorado, Wisconsin, Maryland, Virginia, Utah, Texas, Michigan)
U.S. Regions with Locations:	Central/Midwest, Southern, Mid Atlantic
Locations Outside U.S.:	None

What do six billion people have in common? They love noodles: Thai noodles; stir-fried noodles; macaroni and cheese; linguini; shells; bow ties. Imagine if diners could get all those irresistible noodles in one place. That's what Aaron Kennedy did when he founded Noodles in 1995.

The global noodle shop seemed the ideal restaurant concept for America's evolving dining needs—fast, high-quality, healthy and affordable. The Noodle Shop Co. was founded in 1995 in Boulder, Colorado, when 25 courageous investors entrusted Kennedy's belief that America was ready for the first quick, casual-dining restaurant dedicated to pasta and noodle fare from around the world. Today, the company has more than 63 successful restaurants in Colorado, Illinois, Wisconsin, Minnesota, Maryland, Virginia, Utah, Texas and Michigan. And as long as communities continue to invite Noodles & Company into their neighborhoods, the company plans to continue growing in current and new markets.

Noodles & Company focuses on the customer's total dining experience. In addition to serving bowls of delicious steaming-hot noodles in china bowls, each restaurant features a comfortable dining atmosphere. Natural-colored carpets, recycled wood micro-lam tables, curvaceous suspended noodle fins, cushioned benches and photographs featuring marketplaces from around the globe create an atmosphere that is unusually intimate for a fast and casual-dining concept.

Kennedy also believes that fast and friendly service contributes to the concept's appeal. That is why Noodles & Company offers its customers a venue where they can quickly place their orders at counters, followed by delivery of their orders to sit-down tables in a tip-free zone inside the restaurant or on the patio by staff members who bring freshly prepared noodle cuisine to patrons within minutes.

Noodles are served in china bowls.

Olive Garden

*O*live Garden is a chain
of local restaurants that
offers an Italian dining
experience.

A passion for Italy and an obsession with Italian life that embraced the food, the wine and the genuine hospitality of the country, motivated the founders of Olive Garden to establish a restaurant and culinary institute in Italy to learn from the Italians themselves. The program, which continues to this day and is a large part of its employee culture, sends Olive Garden's culinary managers to the Culinary Institute of Tuscany for training throughout the year. In addition, Olive Garden hosts an annual wine ambassador trip to the vineyards of Italy. The result for Olive Garden guests is a genuine Italian dining experience drawn from the heart of Italy.

Olive Garden is a chain of local restaurants that serves fresh, high-quality Italian food, complemented by a glass of great wine, in a comfortable, home-style setting where guests are welcomed like family and receive warm, friendly service. This passion is fueling Olive Garden's tremendous success. Founded in 1982, Olive Garden is now the leading Italian restaurant in the casual-dining industry.

Olive Garden is a division of Darden Restaurants, the largest casual-dining restaurant company in the world. Darden operates and owns more than 1,200 Red Lobster, Olive Garden, Bahama Breeze and Smokey Bones restaurants in North America.

Parent Company:	Darden Restaurants
Corporate Retail Headquarters:	5900 Lake Ellenor Drive Orlando, FL 32809 (407) 245-2563 (407) 245-4462 Fax http://www.olivegarden.com
Annual Revenue (for Darden Restaurants):	$4.4 billion (2002)
Typical Store/Location Size:	7,000 to 10,000 square feet
U.S. Regions with Locations:	All
Locations Outside U.S.:	Canada

Pasta is served in a comfortable, home-style setting.

On The Border Mexican Grill & Cantina

Experiencing On The Border Mexican Grill & Cantina means feasting on traditional Mexican favorites and mesquite-grilled specialties, which are served in a bold, engaging atmosphere.

On The Border is a special place where the best of two worlds—Mexico and the United States—blend together, their traditions merge, recipes evolve and spices mingle. Flavors depart from the familiar and arrive at the extraordinary. With restaurants in 34 states, On The Border provides unique Mexican food in colorful cantinas with a casual-dining atmosphere all over the country.

In May 1994, Brinker International purchased On The Border. Building on its strong foundation and solid track record and backed by Brinker International's financial strength, On The Border plans to develop 10-plus new restaurants each year.

The restaurant has become a phenomenal success, and today there are more than 100 restaurants throughout the country.

On The Border Mexican Grill & Cantina serves traditional Mexican favorites and mesquite-grilled specialties.

Parent Company:	Brinker International
Corporate Retail Headquarters:	6820 LBJ Freeway Dallas, TX 75240 (972) 980-9917 http://www.ontheborder.com
Annual Revenue (for Brinker International):	$3 billion
Typical Store/Location Size:	5,500 square feet (varies widely)
# of U.S. States with Locations:	34 states
U.S. Regions with Locations:	All
Locations Outside U.S.:	None

Outback Steakhouse

Outback
Steakhouse is an
Australian
steakhouse
concept that
serves its food
and beverages in
an atmosphere
suggestive of the
Australian
outback.

TAKE A WALKABOUT ON OUR WEBSITE.
EXPLORE AND SEE WHAT
THE OUTBACK IS ALL ABOUT.

NO RULES, JUST RIGHT.

Parent Company:	Outback Steakhouse, Inc.
Corporate Retail Headquarters:	2202 N. West Shore Boulevard Tampa, FL 33607 (813) 282-1225 (813) 282-1209 Fax http://www.outback.com

Annual Revenue:	$2,362.1 million (2002)
# of U.S. States with Locations:	49 states
U.S. Regions with Locations:	All
Locations Outside U.S.:	21 countries

Outback Steakhouse is an Australian steakhouse concept, serving dinner only. Although beef and steak items make up a good portion of the menu, the concept offers a variety of chicken, ribs, seafood and pasta dishes served in a casual atmosphere suggestive of the Australian outback.

Outback Steakhouse serves the freshest food possible, using only the highest-quality ingredients. Almost everything is made fresh daily in-house, including the salad dressings, delicious chocolate sauce, croutons and the creamy onion soup. The menu is described as full-flavored and the company is proud that Outback really defines the quality of the food served.

There are currently 783 Outback Steakhouse restaurants across the United States, which are owned and operated by Outback Steakhouse, Inc., headquartered in Tampa, Florida. Founded in 1988, Outback Steakhouse, Inc. is a company of restaurants that includes the Outback Steakhouse, Carrabba's Italian Grill, Fleming's Prime Steakhouse & Wine Bar and Roy's Restaurants.

There are currently restaurants across the United States and in 21 other countries.

Panera Bread

Panera Bread bakery-cafes bring the tradition of freshly baked bread to neighborhoods in cities throughout the country. The enjoyment of fresh bread is at the heart of Panera Bread's success. It is combined with talent, expertise and effort directed toward providing customers with a friendly gathering place in which to relax and share the tradition of fresh-baked bread every day. The cafes also offer a way to extend the tradition to the family table by making its breads available to take home. In every community, cus-

*S*andwiches, bagels, croissants, muffins and pastries are also on the menu.

tomers have responded with enthusiasm, supporting the idea that "fresh bread makes friends."

The highest-quality ingredients and fresh preservative-free doughs are hallmarks of Panera Bread. The baked breads add distinctive freshness, flavor and quality to the cafe menu. The bakery offers more than a dozen varieties of breads as well as bagels, croissants, muffins and pastries.

Panera Bread Company, founded in St. Louis and Kansas City, Missouri, operates and franchises bakery-cafes in 30 states under the Panera Bread and Saint Louis Bread Co. names.

Each bakery-cafe focuses on breads made with all-natural ingredients and a craftsperson's attention to quality and detail. The concept is designed to provide an engaging environment and to meet the key consumer trends of today, specifically the need for an efficient and special dining experience that is more than that offered by traditional fast-food eateries. The menu, operating system and design all enable the bakery-cafe to compete successfully in four key businesses: Breakfast, lunch, daytime "chill-out" periods (the times between breakfast and lunch and between lunch and dinner when customers visit the bakery-cafes to take a break from their daily activities) and take-home bread.

Panera Bread bakery-cafes offer varieties of breads made with all-natural ingredients.

Parent Company:	Panera Bread Company
Corporate Retail Headquarters:	6710 Clayton Road Richmond Heights, MO 63117 (314) 633-7100 (314) 633-7200 Fax http://www.panerabread.com
Annual Revenue:	$277.8 million (2002)
# of U.S. States with Locations:	478 stores in 30 states plus the District of Columbia
U.S. Regions with Locations:	All
Locations Outside U.S.:	None

An engaging environment provides customers with a friendly gathering place to enjoy fresh-baked bread.

P.F. Chang's China Bistro

Founded in 1993, the restaurant has been embraced by diners across the United States.

P.F. Chang's Chinese Bistro serves traditional Chinese food in a high-energy bistro setting.

Parent Company:	P.F. Chang's China Bistro, Inc.
Corporate Retail Headquarters:	15210 North Scottsdale Road Scottsdale, AZ 85254 (602) 957-8986 (602) 957-8998 Fax http://www.pfchangs.com

Annual Revenue:	$422 million (2002)
# of U.S. States with Locations:	80 full-service restaurants in 25 states
U.S. Regions with Locations:	All
Locations Outside U.S.:	None

A sophisticated, contemporary look makes up the design and décor.

Fresh, contemporary and consistently outstanding are the trademarks of P.F. Chang's China Bistro. Founded in 1993, P.F. Chang's is a restaurant that has been embraced by diners across the country. The P.F. Chang's experience is a unique combination of Chinese cuisine, attentive service, wine and tempting desserts all served in a stylish, high-energy bistro.

P.F. Chang's owns and operates 80 full-service restaurants, featuring a blend of high-quality, traditional Chinese cuisine and American hospitality in a sophisticated, contemporary setting.

The cuisine is complemented by a full-service bar, offering an extensive selection of wines, specialty drinks, Asian beers, cappuccino and espresso. Guests receive superior customer service and can enjoy a display kitchen, wok cooking demonstrations and décor that includes mounted life-size terra-cotta replicas of Xi'an warriors and narrative murals depicting 12th-century China.

The company has developed Pei Wei Asian Diner, or Pei Wei, a new concept that caters to a quicker, more casual dining experience, as compared to P.F. Chang's China Bistro. Pei Wei opened its first unit in July 2000, in the Phoenix, Arizona, area. In 2001, four additional units opened—three in the Phoenix, Arizona, area and one in the Dallas, Texas, area. Pei Wei will continue to grow in the coming years.

Pier 1 Imports

*P*ier 1 Imports offers distinct, casual home furnishings at a good value.

*M*erchandise includes indoor and outdoor furniture, among other items.

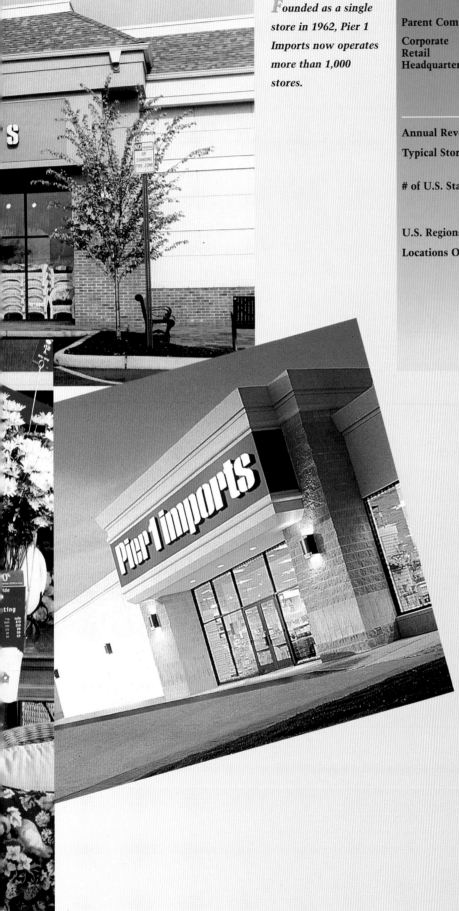

*F*ounded as a single store in 1962, Pier 1 Imports now operates more than 1,000 stores.

Parent Company:	Pier 1 Imports, Inc.
Corporate Retail Headquarters:	301 Commerce Street Fort Worth, TX 76102 (817) 252-8000 (817) 252-8028 Fax http://www.pier1.com
Annual Revenue:	$1.5 billion (2002)
Typical Store/Location Size:	Various, including freestanding, pads and open-air centers
# of U.S. States with Locations:	1,000 stores in 50 states and Puerto Rico and planning to open 115 more stores in fiscal year 2004
U.S. Regions with Locations:	All
Locations Outside U.S.:	Canada, Mexico, U.K.

Pier 1 Imports offers distinct, casual home furnishings at a good value. Its ever-changing collections—as much as 65% of Pier 1's merchandise assortment includes new product introductions each year—are presented in an environment that encourages customers to have fun shopping for their homes.

Pier 1 Imports sells about 5,000 stock keeping units (SKUs) imported from more than 50 countries in more than 1,000 locations in the United States plus about 50 outlets outside of North America. Merchandise includes indoor and outdoor furniture, lamps, vases, baskets, ceramics, dinnerware, candles, paintings and art. Pier 1 Imports is famous for rattan and wood products as well as handcrafted home furnishings.

Founded in 1962 as a single store in San Mateo, CA, Pier 1 Imports is now a publicly owned company.

Pottery Barn, Pottery Barn Kids

*P*ottery Barn is a home furnishings retailer that sells indoor and outdoor furniture, pillows and lamps, among other items.

*T*he first Pottery Barn Kids was opened in 2000.

POTTERYBARN

Pottery Barn operates over 161 stores in the United States.

Parent Company:	Williams-Sonoma, Inc.
Corporate Retail Headquarters:	3250 Van Ness Avenue San Francisco, CA 94109 (415) 421-7900 (415) 616-8359 Fax http://www.potterybarn.com http://www.potterybarnkids.com
Annual Revenue:	$2,086.7 million (2002)
# of U.S. States with Locations:	161 Pottery Barn stores and 63 Pottery Barn Kids stores in 37 states plus the District of Columbia
Locations Outside U.S.:	None

Pottery Barn was a Manhattan–based chain of 21 stores when Williams–Sonoma, Inc. purchased it in 1986. Since then it has evolved the brand into the country's preeminent home-furnishings retailer. In 1994, Pottery Barn introduced the Design Studio, a larger-format store with a wider product selection. These stores also feature worktables where customers can surround themselves with fabric swatches and product photos and plan room arrangements in sketchbooks.

Building on the immediate popularity of the Pottery Barn Kids catalog, Williams-Sonoma opened the first Pottery Barn Kids in September 2000 in Costa Mesa, California. In addition to great kids' furniture and furnishings, it included the launch of the Pottery Barn Kids Baby & Gift Registry.

Red Lobster

Red Lobster operates restaurants in the United States, Canada and Japan.

The menu offers diners seafood at a value price.

Red Lobster's founders have a history of being innovators, explorers and leaders. In 1968, the original Red Lobster was introduced to America in Lakeland, Florida. Company founder Bill Darden had tested his entrepreneurial success on a restaurant concept of a different color, the "Green Frog," along with a 19-year-old protégé, Joe Lee, future president of Red Lobster and current chairman and CEO of Darden Restaurants.

Red Lobster was built on the vision that great service is fundamental to success and on the promise of great-tasting seafood at a value price.

In the early 1970's, Red Lobster expanded throughout the Southeast, establishing itself as the leader not only in chain seafood restaurants but in all of casual dining. The relatively simple box-like buildings, with unadorned facades, reflected founder Bill Darden's simple philosophy. But the casual-dining industry had yet to become the multifaceted pool of choices it is today. Throughout this time, the Red Lobster crew continued to innovate, introducing much of the country to calamari, snow crab and hush puppies, not to mention inventing popcorn shrimp.

By the late 1970's and early 1980's, Red Lobster was 350 restaurants strong. And in 1995, after decades of success and growth, Red Lobster (along with the Olive Garden and later Bahama Breeze and Smokey Bones) was spun into Darden Restaurants, headed up by none other than Joe Lee. The menu

Parent Company:	Darden Restaurants
Corporate Retail Headquarters:	5900 Lake Ellenor Drive Orlando, FL 32809 (407) 245-2563 (407) 245-4462 Fax http://www.redlobster.com
Annual Revenue (for Darden Restaurants):	$4.4 billion (2002)
Typical Store/Location Size:	7,000 to 10,000 square feet
U.S. Regions with Locations:	All
Locations Outside U.S.:	Canada, Japan

changed, becoming broader and more upscale. Casual dining had changed dramatically and, to maintain a leadership position, the restaurants complemented a terrific menu with a new, attractive atmosphere. Architecture took on a new life, and plain boxes gave way to the new wharf-side experience seen today.

There's a new wave rolling at Red Lobster today. President Edna Morris is charting a spectacular new course that has been recognized by diners across the United States, Canada and Japan. The most exciting times are yet to come, as Red Lobster navigates its way to greatness.

Restoration Hardware

Restoration Hardware combines home furnishings with unusual "discovery items."

Functional and decorative hardware is featured in the store.

Parent Company:	Restoration Hardware, Inc.
Corporate Retail Headquarters:	15 Koch Road Corte Madera, CA 94925 (415) 924-1005 (415) 927-9133 Fax http://www.restorationhardware.com

# of U.S. States with Locations:	100 stores in 30 states
U.S. Regions with Locations:	All
Locations Outside U.S.:	Canada

Restoration Hardware commenced business more than 20 years ago as a purveyor of fittings and fixtures for older homes. Since then, the company has evolved into a unique home-furnishings retailer, offering consumers an array of distinctive, high-quality and often hard-to-find merchandise. The stores combine classic, high-quality furniture, lighting, home furnishings and functional and decorative hardware with unusual "discovery items."

Around every corner at Restoration Hardware, shoppers discover something unexpected, yet pleasantly familiar, be it a rich leather chair, satin-nickel fitting for the bath or 464-thread-count bed linens. It's a hardware store unlike any other, filled with products linked by classic design, affordable pricing and an abundance of product information.

The year was 1979 when founder Stephen Gordon was restoring his Queen Anne Victorian house in Eureka, California. After spending endless days tracking down missing bits and pieces of authentic period hardware, lighting fixtures and finishes, Gordon found there were a lot of people with the same problems. He sensed a need in the marketplace, found his true calling in life and opened the first Restoration Hardware store in his home in 1980.

With a proven opening strategy, Restoration Hardware has successfully opened stores in mall, urban and specialty center locations in all regions of the United States, Vancouver, British Columbia, and Toronto, Ontario.

Restoration Hardware believes that its retail concept has broad national appeal and that, as a result, it has significant new store expansion opportunities over the next several years.

Rockfish
Seafood Grill

Rockfish Seafood Grill serves fresh seafood at reasonable prices.

In addition to a distinctive menu and knowledgeable wait staff, the restaurants are comfortable and relaxed.

Parent Company:	Brinker International
Corporate Retail Headquarters:	6820 LBJ Freeway Dallas, TX 75240 (972) 980-9917 http://www.rockfishseafood.com
Annual Revenue: (for Brinker International):	$3 billion
Typical Store/Location Size:	5,500 square feet (varies widely)
# of U.S. States with Locations:	20 locations in 3 states (Texas, Arizona, New Mexico)
U.S. Regions with Locations:	Western, Central/Midwest
Locations Outside U.S.:	None

Rockfish Seafood Grill is a casual neighborhood restaurant, offering fresh, delicious-tasting seafood at reasonable prices for lunch and dinner.

The restaurants are comfortable and relaxed. Whether surrounded by the pine of a mountain fly-fishing lodge or the sleek look reminiscent of a mahogany-and-chrome-trimmed speedboat, guests are enthusiastic about the open kitchens, distinctive menu, creative chefs and knowledgeable wait staff.

The range of menu choices keeps diners coming back for more. Favorites like the shrimp basket, fish taco, stuffed fish, a margarita called the Rock-a-Rita, an 18-ounce beer schooner and an award-winning Mexican-shrimp martini are just a few of the reasons why Rockfish is a favorite.

The fly-fishing theme and casual seafood menu struck a chord with customers, as did the jukebox and open kitchen. Since the first Rockfish opened in February 1998, the company continues to expand.

Rockfish Seafood Grill operates 20 restaurants in Texas, Arizona and New Mexico.

Romano's Macaroni Grill

Romano's Macaroni Grill, the ultimate experience in casual Italian dining, opened in 1988 in a modest stone building in Leon Springs, Texas, near San Antonio. It has set the standard for *Italiano Autentico* ever since.

Phil Romano, one of the most innovative and successful restaurateurs in the United States, drew on boyhood memories of his Italian-American upbringing to create Romano's Macaroni Grill. When guests enter Macaroni Grill, they are immediately met by the sights, sounds and aromas of a traditional Italian kitchen. Gleaming deli cases are filled with fresh seafood, meats and pastas that are served daily at the restaurant. Chefs deftly prepare dish after delectable dish over open flames, in rotisseries and wood-fired ovens. Strings of lights illuminate the dining room's cavernous ceilings and open rafters, and large vases of fresh gladiolas fill the center aisle and give warmth to the exposed stone walls and cement floors. Strolling opera singers serenade diners who enjoy house wine that is poured on the honor system. The tables, which are draped in white linen, are covered with butcher paper and are supplied with crayons that allow guests and children to create their own masterpieces.

Romano's Macaroni Grill offers casual Italian dining, serving seafood, meat and pasta.

In 1989, Dallas, Texas-based Brinker International acquired Romano's Macaroni Grill and began expanding it nationally. The concept has grown to more than 190 restaurants in the United States, Canada, Mexico and the United Kingdom.

The average size of a Romano's Macaroni Grill restaurant is approximately 7,100 square feet, with seating for approximately 280 guests.

Parent Company:	Brinker International
Corporate Retail Headquarters:	6820 LBJ Freeway Dallas, TX 75240 (972) 980-9917 http://www.macaronigrill.com

Annual Revenue (for Brinker International):	$3 billion
Typical Store/Location Size:	7,100 square feet
# of U.S. States with Locations:	40 states plus Puerto Rico
U.S. Regions with Locations:	All
Locations Outside U.S.:	Canada, U.K., Mexico

The tables are covered with butcher paper and supplied with crayons as well as forks and knives so diners can both eat and create their own table-top masterpieces.

Smith & Hawken

Every Smith & Hawken store—from San Diego to the SoHo district in New York City—is a garden-inspired refuge. When customers step inside the store, they find the most extensive collection of garden products. As stated in the companies mission statement: "We believe in the beauty of the garden, whether five acres or one plant."

Upon the first retail store opening in 1984 in Mill Valley, California, Smith & Hawken set out to be the premium provider of unique, high-quality, garden-inspired products. It all began in 1979 when founder John Leavons, a dedicated organic gardener, asked his friends Dave Smith and Paul Hawken, to source and import his favorite hand-forged tools from England.

Smith & Hawken has earned its reputation for its legendary merchandise, which is characterized by integrity, craftsmanship, authenticity and beauty.

Once solely a mail-order company, Smith & Hawken is now a multi-channel retailer of high-quality products marketed through retail stores, catalogs and online. It excels by providing exemplary customer service and support and informational workshops for gardeners of all levels. Smith & Hawken guarantees and stands behind every product it sells. If a product fails to perform to satisfaction, customers may return it within 60 days for an exchange or a refund.

There are currently 51 Smith & Hawken stores throughout the United States. Smith & Hawken is owned by DDJ Capital Management, LLC.

The store's legendary merchandise is characterized by craftsmanship, authenticity and beauty.

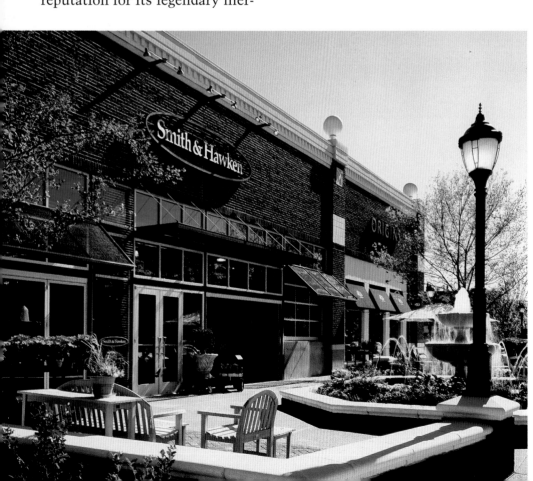

Smith & Hawken's mission statement is: "We believe in the beauty of the garden, whether five acres or one plant."

Smith & Hawken

Parent Company:	DDJ Capital Management, LLC
Corporate Retail Headquarters:	4 Hamilton Landing Novato, CA 94949 (415) 506-3700 (415) 506-3907 Fax http://www.smithandhawken.com

Typical Store/Location Size:	4,500 square feet
# of U.S. States with Locations:	51 stores in 20 states plus the District of Columbia
U.S. Regions with Locations:	All
Locations Outside U.S.:	6

When customers step inside the store, they find an extensive collection of garden products.

Storehouse Furniture

*Storehouse Furniture
believes that
shoppers aren't just
buying furniture,
they are creating a
home.*

torehouse Furniture believes that shoppers aren't just buying furniture, they are creating a home. The furniture shoppers will find at Storehouse is classic and timeless, without being old-fashioned and boring.

Storehouse offers a sophisticated and eclectic blend of unique furnishings for every room of the house. The specialty home-furnishings retailer is known for its distinctive collection of upholstery and furniture for the dining room, bedroom and home office, with styles ranging from contemporary to classic. Storehouse has an extensive in-stock program—500 upholstery fabrics are available at one price, with multiple special-order options—and is well-positioned to respond quickly to its customers' needs.

As a full-line home-furnishings retailer, Storehouse products include a wide range of furniture, home-accent merchandise, accessories, wall décor, lighting and rugs for the living room, den, dining room, bedroom and home office. Products are available through catalogs, online and in 63 stores located in upscale village centers.

A subsidiary of The Rowe Companies, Storehouse is based in Atlanta, Georgia.

Parent Company:	The Rowe Companies
Corporate Retail Headquarters:	Storehouse, Inc. 4200 Perimeter Park South Atlanta, GA 30341 http://www.storehouse.com

# of U.S. States with Locations:	63 stores in 15 states plus the District of Columbia
U.S. Regions with Locations:	East, Mid Atlantic, Southeast, South Central
Locations Outside U.S.:	None

storehouse

Shoppers find furniture that is classic and timeless, without being old-fashioned and boring.

Sur La Table

Established in 1972 in Seattle, Washington's historic Pike Place Farmers' Market, Sur La Table set out to satisfy the growing demands of culinary professionals and home chefs for a reliable source of top-quality cookware and hard-to-find kitchen tools. Known for its cutting-edge merchandise in the culinary industry, Sur La Table was the first retailer on the West Coast to introduce the Cuisinart® food processor. The store quickly became a leader in the marketplace. In response to escalating demand and growing regard for its expertise and wide-ranging inventory, a black-and-white mail-order catalog was published in 1988. At present, the award-winning catalog reaches more than 9 million people worldwide. In 1999, Sur La Table launched an online gift registry and its e-commerce Web site.

A privately held company, Sur La Table's investors include the Behnke family, one of the Northwest's most well-regarded families. Throughout the year, Renée Behnke, President, and a team of expert buyers travel the world in pursuit of distinctive products that make Sur La Table the outstanding emporium it is. Renée and her buyers continue to expand their culinary expertise in order to deliver the highest-quality and most authentic products available. Culinary explorations in the past few years have included France, Italy, England, Portugal, Germany, Morocco, Croatia, Mexico and Vietnam.

Sur La Table is brimming with over 12,000 items from more than 900 vendors worldwide. From an extensive line of French copper cookware directly imported from a sixth-generation family of artisans to many other distinctive brands of cookware, bakeware, small appliances, cutlery, kitchen tools, books, linens, tableware, hard-to-find gadgets and seasonal and specialty foods, the depth of choices is unparalleled.

Many of the company's knowledgeable employees are culinary and hospitality professionals who offer savvy advice and solid expertise about Sur La Table's products, including their use and care.

Sur La Table has expanded its retail presence by recently opening stores in Arizona, California, Colorado, the District of Columbia, Illinois, Nevada, New Jersey, New York, Ohio, Texas, Utah, Virginia and Washington. There are currently approximately 30 Sur La Table stores, averaging 5,500 square feet each.

Parent Company:	Sur La Table, Inc.
Corporate Retail Headquarters:	1938 Occidental Avenue South Seattle, WA 98134 (206) 682-7175 (206) 682-8982 Fax http://www.surlatable.com
Typical Store/Location Size:	5,500 square feet
# of U.S. States with Locations:	30 stores in 29 states plus the District of Columbia
U.S. Regions with Locations:	All
Locations Outside U.S.:	None

There are currently 30 Sur La Table stores in the United States.

Talbots Misses, Talbots Woman, Talbots Woman Petites, Talbots Petites, Talbots Mens, Talbots Kids, Talbots Accessories & Shoes

*B*ehind the signature red door entrance of each Talbots store lies not only classic women's apparel but also a rich and outstanding history of retail. Established in 1947 with a single store location in Hingham, Massachusetts, a suburb of Boston, Talbots expanded its business just one year later when it launched its catalog business. Talbots distributed 3,000 black-and-white fliers to names obtained from *The New Yorker* magazine.

*B*ehind the signature red door at Talbots lies classic apparel.

Today the company's store operations comprise approximately 84% of Talbots overall business, with catalogs representing 16%. By 2002,

*T*albots Kids debuted as a store concept in 1990.

Talbots operated 886 specialty stores throughout the United States, Canada and the United Kingdom and distributed 30 full-color catalogs worldwide. Owned by AEON Co., Ltd., one of Japan's leading retailers and the core company of AEON Group, Talbots' annual revenue in 2001 was $1.6 billion.

As a specialty retailer, cataloger and e-tailer of women's classic apparel, the Talbots collection consists of high-quality sportswear, versatile career separates, casual wear and special-occasion classics. A complementary collection of accessories provides customers with a "head-to-toe" wardrobe.

In a most comprehensive presentation, Talbots offers a number of concepts. The company's core business revolves around **Talbots Misses,** which includes an assortment of clothes in sizes from 4 to 20 in stores that average approximately 3,700 square feet. **Talbots Petites** sells sizes from 2 to 16 and is in every Talbots Misses store, except where sales generated have warranted a separate Talbots Petites store of approximately 2,000 square feet.

Launched initially in the catalog, **Talbots Kids** debuted as a store concept in 1990. The assortment includes colorful, wearable clothing for girls and boys in sizes from 2 to 16. In the approximately 2,600-square-foot store, a fun play area complete with toys and videos is featured. A catalog success, **Talbots Accessories & Shoes** were introduced as stores in 1995, each approximately 1,300 square feet.

High-quality clothing designed to fit women who wear sizes from 12W to 24W can be found at **Talbots Woman** stores, complementing the successful existing catalog business from this customer group. In 2001, **Talbots Woman Petites**, offering sizes for fuller-figured women who are five feet four inches tall and under, were added to the collection.

Parent Company:	AEON Co., Ltd.
Corporate Retail Headquarters:	One Talbots Drive Hingham, MA 02043 (781) 749-7600 (781) 741-4369 Fax http://www.talbots.com
Annual Revenue:	$1.6 billion (2001)
Typical Store/Location Size:	4,110 square feet gross 3,130 square feet selling
# of U.S. States with Locations:	47 plus the District of Columbia
U.S. Regions with Locations:	All
Locations Outside U.S.:	U.K. and Canada

In October 2002, a new concept, **Talbots Mens**, was launched via catalog. The company is monitoring results and anticipates opening one to three Talbots Mens stores in 2003.

Stores operate in the United States, Canada and the United Kingdom.

Through three distribution channels that include specialty stores, catalogs and online shopping, Talbots is most deserving of its distinguished red door entrance.